The Secret's Out:

Why You Need To Feed Your Dog a Raw Food Diet

Amy Marshall

Dedicated to Bear.

If only I knew this information sooner.

Acknowledgements

Thank you to Brendan, my biggest supporter and fan, for always listening to my dreams, visions, and plans, and motivating me to pursue them.

Thank you to the Marshall and Rabadi families for supporting my hobby, even when you didn't understand why on earth I was feeding my dog raw meat.

Thank to the raw dog food brands and natural health businesses who supported me and Primal Pooch, especially Lisa Ayotte of Soul'y Raw, my very first blog supporter.

Special thanks to Rodney Habib for taking time out of his insane schedule to share his knowledge with me. Thanks also for showing us how many dog owners are committed to providing their pets better quality food, and how bloggers can make a difference.

Thank you to Kathryn Kos of Primal Bliss for pushing me to publish my eBook and giving me the encouragement and information I needed to take the first step.

To Mark Sisson: while I don't know you personally, I feel compelled to thank you for starting me down this path. If it weren't for your book, Primal Blueprint, I may have never discovered a canine ancestral diet.

Thanks to my editor, Daniel Swensen, and designer, Milana Marinkovic, for helping me turn my vision into a reality.

Last but not least, thank you to all the PrimalPooch.com readers who continue to read, devour, and share my content with other dog owners. There's much more to come!

Table of Contents

Intro

Conclusion

*"Life doesn't allow us to go back and fix what we
have done wrong in the past, but it does allow us to
live each day better than the last."*

WELCOME TO THE
BEGINNING OF THE END

Are you sick and tired of watching your dog suffer from
health issues? Or do you simply want to prevent health
problems from arising in the future?

If so, then this book is for you.

Years of research and hours of reading have been compiled
into this comprehensive guide that answers the WHY behind
raw feeding as a practice.

The next eleven in-depth, informative chapters outline
everything from:

- Your dog's ancestors,
- Canine evolution and domestication,
- The birth of pet food,
- The problem with traditional dry and wet dog food today.

If you know you could be doing better with your dog's diet, then what are you waiting for?

Save time and frustration trying to navigate this confusing and complex topic alone. I'll outline everything you need to know to make better diet and nutrition decisions for your dog.

Your only risk:

This might be the beginning of the end – of pet food, that is.

PART
ONE

Canine History & Evolution

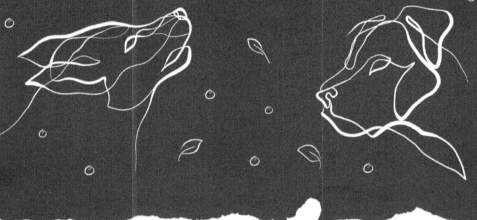

*"We can only know where we're going
if we know where we've been"*

-Maya Angelou

Is it hard to picture your dog as animal that once came from the wild?

Dogs have a way of acting like mini-people. Packed full of personality, quirks, and character, they blend seamlessly into our lives. Because they seem so human, it's sometimes easy for us to forget their long and impressive histories.

Why should we care about canine history?

Because to understand what dogs *should* eat, we must first understand where they came from and what they are at their most basic level.

You don't need to be a field scientist or an animal researcher to comprehend this material.

Take a step back into history with me as we rediscover the origins of the domestic dog. Trust me, it's worth knowing.

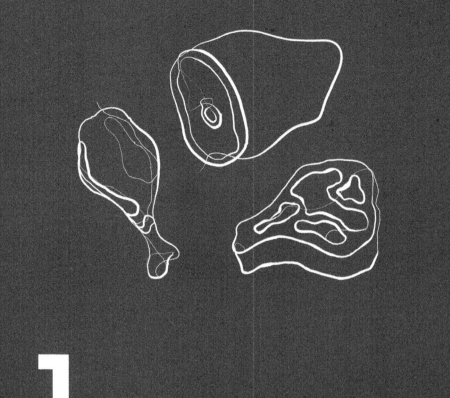

1 WOLF FOOD

Maybe you didn't give the wolf much thought before you learned about this thing called "raw feeding."

Why would you?

But now that you're interested in more healthful and *natural* dietary options for your dog, it's time to visit his or her roots.

Your dog's relatives are the key to this nutritional puzzle.

To start this educational raw feeding journey, we're going to recap dietary habits of the noble wolf.

Let's begin.

The Research

There is no way to know for *sure* what the wolf's diet consists of. Depending on the species of wolf and the wolf's natural environment (geography, climate, etc.) it may vary considerably.

Fortunately for us, there's a wealth of research on the topic.

Here's what we know for sure:

1. Modern taxonomy classifies wolves as carnivores.
2. Wolves are hunters and scavengers.

Carnivores Defined

By definition[1], a carnivore is "an organism that derives its energy and nutrient requirements from a diet consisting *mainly* of or *exclusively* of animal tissue, whether through predation or scavenging."

Carnivores mostly eat a diet consisting of:

- Muscle meat
- Connective tissue like ligaments and tendons
- Organs
- Bone
- Hide, hair, or fur

Predation and Scavenging

Predation and scavenging are feeding behaviors.

Predation is another world for hunting[2]. Like most carnivores, wolves are efficient hunters. Their heightened senses and powerful bodies allow them to track, stalk and kill prey.

But hunting is hard work.

And it's not free from injury or risk.

For wolves, conserving calories and finding food are top priorities. That's why wolves also scavenge.

Scavenging can include eating animals that have died of natural causes, digging through the leftovers from another predator's kill, or consuming non-animal foods.

Wolves tend to engage in scavenging behaviors when fresh meat is unavailable, especially during denning, pack activities, and after being unsuccessful in making a kill.

But that's not to say wolves won't scavenge if the opportunity presents itself.

What Do Wolves Eat?

Wolves seem to prefer[3] large hoofed mammals (called ungulates). This can include deer, elk, moose, caribou, bison, and mountain goats[4].

But this doesn't rule out fish and small prey.

Wolves are opportunistic[5]. Beavers, rabbits, birds and other smaller animals are less frequent, but remain a dinner option[6].

Wolves have even been spotted catching fish in places like Alaska and Western Canada. Some research[7] suggests that when fresh salmon is available, wolves may reduce deer hunting and focus on fishing instead.

How much of a prey animal does a wolf eat?

Wolves make good use of a prey animal's carcass, consuming what's edible and leaving only what they can't handle.

In the case of small animals, the entire carcass may be devoured. With larger animals, some hair, hide, and weight bearing bones often get left behind, since they're too dense to eat. On average, a wolf will consume 80-100% of their prey's body.

Do Wolves Eat Non-Animal Foods?

Though wolves are classified as carnivores, they've been observed eating plants. This can include a *small* amount of seasonal fruit and some grasses.

Regardless, plants have not been proven to be a significant part of their diet, and the findings vary by researcher.

Many people question the true nature of plant-based food sources in the diet of the wolf.

The verdict is still out.

As with any wild animal, diet depends on the availability and even vulnerability of prey in their area. Some species of wolves may rely on scavenging plant-based items more heavily than others.

Wolves Are Built to Last

The hardiness of the wolf has been documented throughout history.

Wolves and wild candids come equipped with strong survival mechanisms. This allows them to survive extreme conditions and endure when times are tough.

One example of this is the wolf's ability to go long periods of time without a fresh kill. They have a superior capacity for fasting, and can survive scavenging or eating other types of foods.

Studies of wolves in Yellowstone have documented instances where the wolf's prey consumption dropped 25% in summer, when other food was available.

Other research has cited a wolf that survived a ten-week period without fresh meat in the winter.

How did the animal survive?

By living on previously scavenged carcasses consisting mostly of dried bone and hide.

Why Should You Care?

Many of you reading this book may already know what wolves eat.

If you're a Discovery Channel fan, you've likely had a front row seat to a wolf's hunting and eating habits. So, this probably isn't new information. But it's important we start from the beginning and paint a complete picture.

Next, we'll cover the evolution from the wolf to the domestic dog.

Key Takeaway:

The wolf is a carnivore that hunts and scavenges for food. While their diet may vary, the one constant is that it is primarily meat based.

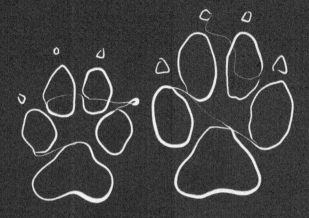

2 EVOLUTION OF THE WOLF

So why should you care about the evolution of the wolf?

Consider this:

If you understand *how* the wolf evolved to the domestic dog, your knowledge of the canine species improves. This insider's view can provide new insight on how to better care for your dog.

So, let's recap evolution.

When Did the Wolf Evolve into the Dog?

If reading dense scientific studies are your idea of fun, then break out your library card. There's no shortage of material on the subject, either in the library or online.

But here's the short version:

It's believed wolves began to evolve into dogs between 18,800 - 32,100 years ago.[8][9] Other sources claim domestication happened as early as 40,000 years ago and as late as 12,000 years ago.

Let's Put This into Perspective

This timeframe falls during the Paleolithic and Mesolithic eras – the days of cavemen and hunter-gatherers.

Your ancestors were painting on cave walls and making the ancient artifacts you've viewed in museums or read about in history books. We existed with creatures like the Woolly Rhinoceros and had not yet developed agriculture.

In other words, man and dog have existed together for a *very* long time.

Now, let's figure out how man and dog first became friends.

How Did Wolves Evolve?

Early history has a lot of gaps, so theories vary on this point. There are several schools of thought:

1. Wolf Pup Theory

This hypothesis states that early man took wolf pups from their den and raised them with humans. Much like we raise a puppy today, these wolf pups were supposedly fed, trained and tamed by early man.

This theory may leave us warm and fuzzy inside, but many doubt its validity[10].

Some claim early man would not have been able to steal wolf pups successfully, since they were fiercely protected and guarded by pack members.

It's possible early man found orphaned wolf pups to raise and domesticate, but there's uncertainty that first generation wolf pups could have been domesticated so quickly.

It takes hundreds to thousands of years to domesticate an animal successfully. It's not as simple as raising a wolf pup into a dog that's comfortable, submissive and tame around humans.

2. Hunting Help Theory

Another hypothesis is that early man may have followed and learned from wolves as they tracked game.

The wolves' sense of smell and other animal instincts were more powerful and successful in hunting, and early peoples could have used this to their advantage.

When it comes to this theory, some disagree that early man needed hunting tips.

Early civilizations were quite successful hunters and even had a reputation for wiping out other carnivorous animals altogether (like saber-toothed cats and giant hyenas).

3. Wolves Domesticated Themselves

Many now theorize wolves domesticated themselves[11].

Less aggressive wolves that were curious enough to inspect the permanent settlements of man were likely to find scraps, waste, and leftovers to feed on.

Over time, as wolves ventured closer to humans, they may have become more comfortable and friendly around them. Wolves that lingered in human presence could have passed along behavioral traits in successive generations.

Likewise, this may have caused people to view wolves differently and develop a mutually beneficial relationship. This could have sparked the long and gradual process of domestication.

Answers Are Not Set in Stone

When and how this process began will continue to be a subject of controversy. We can only speculate and make educated guesses.

Perhaps there was no single way the wolf became domesticated. It could have been a combination of the above theories that brought us the domesticated dog we love today.

What matters is that evolution happened. Thousands of years later, dogs are still by our side.

How Does Evolution Work?

Most of us are aware of the term evolution. It's the theory that explains how living things change over a long period.

Let's take a look at the basics of evolution.

Natural Selection is the vehicle behind evolution. This is how it works:

1. Genetic diversity exists in all populations. It could be a physical or behavioral trait, like size or aggressiveness.

2. Many of these variations are neutral, but when one of these qualities affects an animal's ability to survive, it becomes important.

3. Animals that have a beneficial quality, like better camouflaging from predators for example, will survive and reproduce more often. This increases the frequency of those traits in the population.

4. As those beneficial traits become more common, the animal population changes overall and becomes better suited to its environment.

With wolves, we suspect those who were friendlier and less suspicious of humans benefited.

Perhaps they found food more easily and thus lived longer. In turn, this may have affected certain aspects of the developmental process. Animals that were more puppy-like in behavior were bred more often, leading to physical characteristics like coat color and floppy ears.

Wolves began to change over time as they interacted with humans.

The rest, as they say, is history.

But That's Not All...

That's evolution in a nutshell. It's the natural, survival-of-the-fittest factor.

But it's only *half* of the equation in the larger picture of the domestication of dogs[12]. Let's see what happened once we stepped in and influenced the process.

Key Takeaway:

Once wolves began interacting with humans, they slowly began to change.

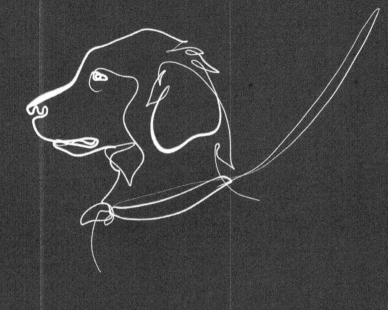

3 DOMESTICATION OF THE DOG

At this point, you may be thinking: "Is this lesson on domestication truly necessary?"

I think so, and I'll tell you why.

Canine domestication is a major piece of the puzzle of why so many well-intentioned canine caregivers go awry with nutrition.

In this chapter, we'll cover everything you need to know about domestication, and what that means in terms of the two species involved:

The wolf and the dog.

Evolution vs. Domestication

Remember, evolution[13] is a natural process that explains how animals change over time.

Domestication is just the opposite. It's *man-made*. It's a process where people genetically modify plants and animals for traits that are advantageous.

Historically, there are three main reasons humans domesticate animals.

1. To create a ready food source,
2. To harness animals for work,
3. Companionship.

Once we learned dogs had tremendous working ability, we began domesticating dogs to work for us.

Say Hello To Artificial Selection and Selective Breeding

As dogs evolved, early man identified the potential in dogs and stepped in to further advance the process.

Darwin called this *artificial* selection.

It's similar to natural selection, but instead of letting nature take its course, people (rather than Mother Nature) select the traits that will continue.

Who benefits?

With artificial selection[14], it's no longer survival of the fittest, but more like "what works best for us?"

The traits chosen may not benefit the animal at all, and often don't. Instead, the characteristics chosen are those directly benefiting people.

This is also known as *selective* breeding.

As wolves slowly domesticated themselves (becoming tamer and changing in physical appearance), man began breeding dogs with the most useful traits.

Over time, humans began to favor certain attributes over others and used artificial selection to create different types of dogs.

Artificial selection created the domestic dogs we have today.

How Do Wild and Domesticated Animals Differ?

This is the key point:

Most of us look at wild and domesticated animals as completely different species.

They're not.

Not only do we treat them differently, **we feed them differently.**

Throughout history, humans have domesticated all kinds of animals, including dogs, horses, and honey bees.

What's interesting is that these animals belong to the same species as their closest wild relatives, and have essentially the same genetic makeup.[15]

The only differences lie in their *appearance* and *behavior*.

In other words, they're virtually the same animal, but with a makeover and an attitude adjustment.

What Happens to An Animal During Domestication?

Because domesticated animals aren't free to choose their

mate, people *breed* the traits or appearance they desire.

Over the course of several generations, this causes the body to transform.

Many domesticated animals become smaller than their wild ancestors. Some have floppier ears, smaller teeth, shorter snouts, or curlier tails. Others gain white markings and different color patterns.

It's believed these physical traits are genetically linked to gentle behavior.

Another aspect is submissiveness. The ancestors of most domesticated animals are social creatures by nature, often living in groups in the wild. In other words, a tendency to submit to others already exists within domestic animals.

Generations of selective breeding have increased this tendency and encouraged the animals to let people take the lead.

Lastly, we have "wildness" of the animal.

Since domesticated animals are cared for, they lose some of their "wildness" and generally become more docile than their rugged cousins.

These are just a few of the ways wild and domesticated animals differ.

Now, let's see how it played out in the case of dogs.

The Selective Breeding of Dogs

Most dogs come from a narrow set of ancestors.

But here's what happened once humans took the wheel and domesticated the dog:

People used selective breeding to create dogs that worked

or served a specific purpose. This could have been herding, hunting, protection, or some other practical skill set.

Dogs worked for man like this for thousands of years. As time went on, civilization became more advanced. Dogs became popular not only as working animals, but as *companions*.

During the late Victorian era, dog breeds proliferated.

Dog breeding was quite trendy at this time. In fact, most modern breeds originated in the Victorian era. Soon, dogs were regarded as luxury items and status symbols. People attempted to produce dogs that were superior in either appearance or function.

Years of selective breeding resulted in the "artificial evolution" of dogs into many different types and categories based, on their early uses.

This is why dogs come in such a diverse variety today.

There are at least a hundred and fifty different dog breeds, and this reflects a purposeful and intense period of interbreeding over the past century or so.

This explains how the Chihuahua and Great Dane can be the same species; yet bear no resemblance to one another. Or why bulldogs have heads so massive they're unable to give birth naturally.

Did you know bulldogs require Caesarean sections to get puppies through the birth canal? Obviously, this trait is not favored by nature. Modern veterinary medicine allows this to continue, and it's something we chose to artificially create for the sake of appearances.

Today, dogs are so diverse; it's easy to forget they spawned from the same animal thousands of years ago.

But looks aren't everything.

Genetics Tell a Convincing Story

Despite physical appearances and behavior, dogs remain shockingly similar to the wolf in terms of:

- Genetics
- Anatomy
- Physiology

Under the hood, a dog and wolf are virtually the same.

How?

Dogs and wolves are so closely related that the dog is not a different species entirely, but a *subspecies* of the wolf. They share an almost identical genetic blueprint.

Their DNA differs by as little as 0.2%.

In fact, dogs and wolves are so similar; they can mate and produce viable offspring, which is evident by the number of wolf hybrids seen today.

Here are some other similarities:

- Their gestation period is the same
- Pups are born blind and deaf
- Shedding patterns are equal
- Both animals take part in the same behaviors (like vocalization, scent rolling and grooming)
- Wolves use certain communication cues (vocalizations, body posture, tail movement, etc.) to convey intent and info to other members of the pack. Dogs use the same communication cues with other dogs and human family members

Are there notable differences between a dog and a wolf?

Of course.

But they tend to lie in appearance and behavior, not with internal bodily functions.

There are even claims that histologists and histo-pathologists cannot tell the internal organs of canines and wolves apart.

The point?

We've been conditioned to believe dogs are separate. They're not.

It's true; dogs are not the same as wild Wolves.

But they ARE *domesticated* Wolves.

However you choose to cut it, dogs are a subspecies of the wolf. While they've evolved over the years, their digestive tracts and nutritional needs likely haven't changed much.

What we feed dogs should be *practical*, but it shouldn't stray too far from what's species-appropriate.

The Next Leg of the Journey

If you've struggled to figure out what you should be feeding your dog, then Part II will cover the question at the forefront of everyone's mind.

It's the proverbial elephant in the room in the never-ending raw feeding debate:

Is your dog a carnivore or an omnivore?

If this question is of no concern to you, feel free to skip ahead to Part III. Otherwise, get comfortable and settle in for the next leg of this educational and hopefully eye-opening journey.

> ### Key Takeaway:
> While the dog may have changed on the outside, internally he's still essentially a wolf.

PART

The Carnivore / Omnivore Saga

TWO

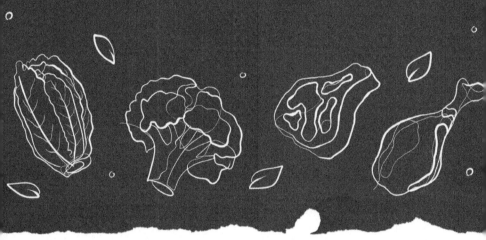

"It is better to debate a question without settling it than to settle a question without debating it"

-Joseph Joubert

Let's recap. So far we've:

- Learned that wolves are carnivores.
- Reviewed a sample menu for the average wolf in the wild.
- Wrapped our minds around the concept of evolution and artificial selection that created the dogs we know today.

In the quest for the most natural diet for dogs, many dog owners find themselves running into the same roadblock:

Is my dog a carnivore or omnivore?

Sources vary on the subject, and a long-standing controversy surrounds the topic.

To some, the answer is inconsequential. To others, it's everything.

How do you determine the optimal diet for your dog if you can't find consistent information?

For answers, we go back to the history and science books.

I can't promise to settle this age-old debate. But together, we can:

- Explore the differences between carnivores, omnivores, and herbivores.
- Review the evidence.
- Arrive at a logical conclusion

We may never find a definitive answer, but we can come up with a strong theory, and that's good enough.

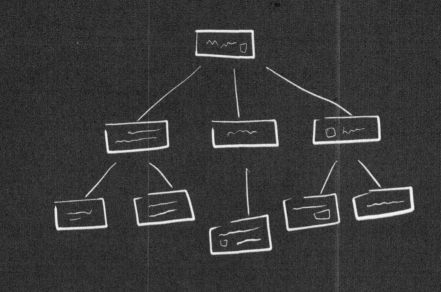

4 ANIMAL CLASSIFICATION, SIMPLIFIED

Before moving on, we're going to revisit some elementary science concepts. These ideas can help us in our quest to understand what types of foods dogs were designed to eat.

Let's kick it off with animal classification.

Animal classification helps us understand how living organisms are related. There are billions of living things on earth. To making studying them easier, scientists needed to come up with a way to organize them.

Taxonomy is the study of animal classification.

This practice can be dated back to ancient civilizations, but the true, scientific attempt to classify organisms began in the eighteenth century.

Since Darwin's time, this biological classification of living things reflects the evolutionary relationships and distances between organisms. All creatures today came from common ancestors in the past so, we're essentially studying the family trees of all living things.

If you plan to study where your dog came from and what your dog should eat, this is a great place to start.

Taxonomy Basics

Taxonomy[16] organizes living things into seven main groups (taxons). These groups descend from large to small, and many have their own subgroups. Since this isn't a research paper, we'll keep it simple.

Here's how it works:

1. Kingdom

Kingdoms consist of millions of organisms in each category: animals, plants, protists, fungi, and bacteria.

Dogs are animals, so they fall under the Kingdom: *Animalia*.

2. Phylum

Phylums are organized with anatomical structure and skeletal features in mind.

Dogs have backbones (vertebrates) and so belong to the Phylum: *Chordata*.

3. Class

Classes organize phylums by traits that further distinguish

animals. For example, the Chordata phylum splits into groups like mammals, fish, amphibians, and reptiles.

Mammals share several important characteristics. They're warm-blooded, they feed their young with milk, and they have hair.

Dogs fall in the Class: *Mammalia*.

4. Order

Orders define classes even further, and the classifications become slightly less distinct.

For example, mammals are divided into about 19 different orders. Each order shares similar characteristics, such as meat-eaters, insect-eaters, pouched animals, primates, rodents and so forth.

Dogs are in the meat-eater club, or Order: *Carnivora*.

5. Family

Families are groups of animals with a lot in common. For example, the Carnivora Order breaks into families like cats, dogs, bears, weasels, etc.

To no one's surprise, dogs are part of the dog family, also called *Canidae*.

6. Genus

Genus is a relatively small group of animals with extremely similar features. Dogs are part of the Genus: *Canis*. This includes wolves, domestic dogs, coyotes, and jackals.

7. Species

At the end of the taxonomy hierarchy, each individual species is named after their unique features and characteristics.

Species names are in Latin so they can be understood worldwide, and consist of two words. The first word is the Genus and the second word is the Species.

Classification of The Wolf & Domestic Dog

The wolf looks something like this:

Kingdom: Animalia
Phylum: Chordata
Class: Mammalia
Order: Carnivora
Family: Canidae
Genus: Canis
Species: **Canis Lupus**

And the domestic dog:

Kingdom: Animalia
Phylum: Chordata
Class: Mammalia
Order: Carnivora
Family: Canidae
Genus: Canis
Species: **Canis Lupus Familiaris**

And there you have it:

An overview used by scientists all over the world to measure the similarities and differences between animals.

Did you see that dogs are part of the meat-eating family of animals? Did you also notice how dogs and wolves separate at the very *last* grouping in the taxonomy system?

You won't find many people arguing this classification.

But if you bring up the topic of a natural canine diet...

Arguments ensue.

Many members of the medical and/or veterinary communities refute this classification, claiming dogs are in fact, omnivores.

It seems contradictory to disagree with the foundation of animal classification used universally around the world. Like many others before me, I prefer to align with the common sense approach that's worked for scientists for over two hundred years.

For the sake of argument, let's review the differences between carnivores, omnivores and herbivores next.

Key Takeaway

For over two hundred years, dogs have been classified as meat-eaters in the modern taxonomy system used by scientists all over the world.

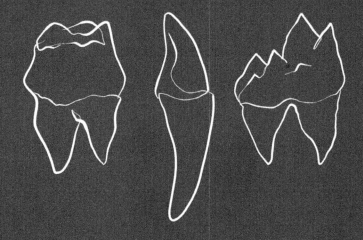

Modern day taxonomy says your dog is a *carnivore.*

But your brand of dog food and your veterinarian may say the opposite: your dog is an *omnivore.*

Talk about confusing!

Here's what science says.

Most mammals overwhelmingly fall into one of these three categories, based on the common characteristics they share:

- Carnivore
- Omnivore
- Herbivore

Let's review them together.

When we're done, you'll see which group makes the most sense for your dog, and you can make an informed decision about your dog's nutrition.

How Animals Find Food

When it comes to locating food, these groups of animals have different approaches:

Carnivores hunt.

- Predatory animals expend a tremendous amount of energy to sustain themselves.

- They track, stalk, chase, and kill their prey, sometimes over long distances. As you might imagine, this lifestyle demands a lot of physical exertion.

- Food is not served to predators. They must work for it.

Herbivores graze.

- Herbivores feed on plant matter already present in nature.

- They may walk or travel to find what they're looking for, but vegetation doesn't need to be hunted.

Omnivores do both.

- Omnivores expend energy according to what they're eating: using more energy and intensity when hunting, and taking it easy when grazing.

Animals Have a Style of Eating

Carnivores devour.

• After a kill, predators waste no time in eating their dinner.

• Carnivores tend to *gorge* themselves, consuming a large quantity of food quickly. They eat as much as possible because they don't know when their next meal is coming and competition is fierce.

• This is hard work.

• Strong neck and jaw muscles are needed to catch, kill, rip, shred, and tear through prey.

• After eating, carnivores take a much-needed rest.

Herbivores graze.

• Herbivores eat slowly but continuously throughout the day.

• Food is readily available, so there's no sense of urgency or competition. While eating is more leisurely for this group of animals, it can be time-consuming and slow.

• Herbivorous animals generally need to eat a large volume of plant matter to sustain their nutritional needs. Slower release of energy means herbivores may need to adopt a lifestyle that minimizes energy expenditure.

Omnivores mix it up.

• Omnivores fall in the middle of the spectrum. They adapt their style of eating to the type of food they're consuming.

Tools for Mealtime:

What physical equipment do animals possess to assist them during mealtime?

Carnivores and omnivores have claws.

While they may vary in size, carnivores and omnivores have sharp, elongated, or pointed claws.

This allows them to capture or kill prey even if a major portion of their diet is plant based. Without these tools, they'd have a hard time including meat in their diet.

Herbivores have hooves or hoof-like feet.

Herbivores typically possess either hooves or flattened nails, for purposes such as traction and sure-footedness.

Herbivores don't need claws, because they don't hunt.

Jaw Bone Functions

Believe it or not, the jaw does more than hold teeth in place. An animal's jaw serves a specific function.

An herbivore's jaw has a wide range of motion.

Herbivores tend to have smaller mouths with muscular tongues to move food around. They also have unbelievable range of motion in their jaws.

This allows them to chew, chew, and chew all day long.

A carnivore's jaw has limited range of motion.

Carnivores don't have the same range of motion in their jaws.

A carnivore's jaw moves mostly vertically. The jaw clamps

to grab and tear meat, then hinges open wide to gulp food.

Carnivores are not actually chewing their food, since they can't move their jaws side-to-side. A single hinge-type joint exists for swallowing chunks of meat whole.

Omnivore jaws vary.

Bears are omnivores, but their jaws resemble a carnivore's. So they're able to apply the force necessary to kill prey.

Humans are also omnivores, but we share a weaker and more mobile herbivore-styled jaw. This allows us a sideways grinding motion, similar to other plant eaters.

Those Pearly Whites

Teeth hold one of the biggest clues into the natural diet of an animal.

When scientists and paleontologist examine fossils, teeth are often the first point of reference to determine an extinct animal's probable diet.

The size, shape and dentition (the way teeth fit together) are all descriptive of an animal's diet.

Herbivores have blunt teeth.

Herbivores have rounded, flat teeth.

Flat teeth are necessary for grinding plant material into finer pieces.

An herbivore's front teeth (incisors) pick plant material. Their long tongues push this material to the back of the mouth for grinding by the back teeth (molars).

Carnivores have sharp, pointed teeth.

Long, sharp, and pointed teeth are designed to penetrate deep into prey and tear meat from bone. Carnivores also have an interlocking aspect to their teeth. They fit tightly together and lock in place, which makes ripping flesh easier.

With these animals there is no grinding. Bone is crushed. Meat is sliced, torn, or held in place with incisors and canines (the longest teeth).

Meat and bone is further broken down by a few chomps with the back teeth (molars) before it's swallowed.

Omnivores may have both.

For omnivores, teeth often vary by species.

A bear, for example, has many sharp pointed teeth in the front, but possesses flat molars in the back.

Humans have mostly dull, rounded teeth and flat molars but we've retained just four pointed, canine teeth.

Making an Animal's Mouth Water: Let's Talk About Saliva

There are also differences among saliva in these three groups of animals.

The sight or smell of food stimulates an animal's salivary glands to secrete saliva. This fluid typically moistens and softens food, making it easier to swallow.

Depending on the animal, the saliva may also contain digestive enzymes.

Herbivores have salivary amylase.

In herbivores, saliva contains the digestive enzyme *amylase.*

Herbivores chew their food thoroughly to ensure mixing with amylase. This jump-starts the digestive process by breaking down starchy carbohydrates into simple sugars before entering the stomach.

Some omnivores also produce salivary amylase but it depends on the animal.

Carnivores do not have salivary amylase.

Carnivores don't mix their food with saliva in the same way an herbivore does. They're not chewing to mix their food with digestive enzymes. Carnivores bite off large chunks of meat and swallow them whole, using saliva for lubrication.

The amylase enzyme is secreted in the body, just further down in the digestive tract.

The Stomach Doesn't Lie

After food passes through the mouth and the esophagus, we find more differences within the stomach:

Herbivores generally have smaller stomachs.

In herbivores, the stomach accounts for approximately less than 30% of the overall volume of the digestive tract, and has a smaller capacity.

Some herbivores (such as cows) even have multiple chambers within their stomachs.

All stomachs are acidic to a degree, because they help us break down our food. The stomach of an herbivore has a pH of 4-5 when there's food inside.

To put this into better perspective, liquids with an equivalent pH include black coffee, tomato juice, and acid rain.

Carnivores generally have larger stomachs with a greater capacity.

Compared to their overall digestive tract, a carnivore's stomach accounts for approximately 60-70% of the total volume.

A large stomach volume is a necessity; since these animals might average only one kill per week. When they do get a kill, they take in as much meat as possible.

When carnivores have food in their stomachs, the pH is less than or equal to 1 – a value comparable to battery acid or concentrated sulfuric acid.

A low pH level is required to break down protein and kill dangerous bacteria found in decaying flesh.

Omnivores are in between.

Many omnivores share a similar stomach setup with carnivores, but have also developed gastrointestinal tract adaptations to herbivorous diets.

Stomach capacity varies.

Many omnivores are similar to carnivores, with the stomach taking up 60-70% of the digestive tract. However, the human stomach takes up 21-27% of total digestive tract volume.

The same goes for the pH scale. Select omnivores fall around a pH of 1 and some around a pH of 4 or 5.

Intestines: The Last Pass of the Digestive Tract

After the stomach, food passes through the small intestines

and large intestines (a.k.a. the colon). This is where water and nutrients are absorbed and waste is prepared for elimination.

Again, we see some differences in the intestines of these animals.

Herbivores have longer intestines and more elaborate guts.

Plant foods consist of large amounts of indigestible, cellulosic fibers. Animals that consume plants with a high proportion of cellulose must be able to convert the indigestible cellulose into digestible nutrients.

They do this through the process of *fermentation.*

In simple terms, fermentation is digestion with the help of bacterial enzymes. To maximize digestion, most herbivores have evolved with specialized guts that contain areas for plant foods to ferment.

Fermentation of plant material can take hours, making digestion and transit time much slower.

Carnivores have short and simple guts.

Meat is easily digestible, relative to plants.

This is why a carnivore's guts are shorter and less complex than herbivores or omnivores.

No fermentation or elaborate digestive processes are required to extract nutrition from their diet. Protein and fats provide a quick and concentrated source of nutrients for the body.

In the carnivore's colon, a large population of healthy bacteria thrives, participating in immune system function and minimizing the presence of dangerous bacteria.

Omnivores have flexible guts.

Omnivores generally have medium length intestines. They fall in the middle, shorter than the herbivore but longer than the carnivore.

An omnivore's digestive tract provides the flexibility to digest both vegetation and animal protein.

Where Does Your Dog Fit?

This is by no means a comprehensive list of all the anatomical differences among carnivores, omnivores and herbivores.

But hopefully it provides a nice overview.

From here, we can start to determine where your dog fits in, and what types of foods may have been natural for them.

Some of you may not be convinced.

Based on this list of criteria, it's clear there's no fine line between carnivore and omnivore. So let's dive deeper into the question:

Is the dog a carnivore or omnivore?

Key Takeaway

Animals were built to eat and digest a specific type of diet, and digestive processes vary accordingly.

6 ARE DOGS CARNIVORES OR OMNIVORES

Like most people, you've probably heard many different beliefs about what your dog was *built* to eat and what they should be eating.

As with parenting, opinions are plentiful. It's not always easy to decipher which viewpoint is worth adopting.

The good news?

You're capable of making your own educated decision, without getting bogged down in debates and without abandoning the idea of a natural and authentic canine diet.

Let's go over the arguments on both sides of the fence.

Looking to Genes for Answers

Pro-Omnivore Argument:

Those in favor of the omnivore angle claim dogs are genetically adapted to eat vegetation and grains.

For good reason.

In 2013, research into the genetic changes that accompanied the transformation of wolves into domestic dogs discovered[17] dogs have ten genes related to starch digestion and fat metabolism.

Does this means dogs are undeniably omnivores?

Not necessarily.

But it's hard to deny dogs are better adapted to eat plant matter compared to their wild cousins.

After eating a grain-based diet for decades, dogs have likely developed the ability to process some starch.

If animals weren't able to adjust at some degree to changes in their environment (diet included), they would die, and the species would eventually become extinct.

Supporters of the omnivore argument also argue that similarities in DNA sequences between animals isn't the end all be all. For example, human DNA is 95% identical to chimpanzees.[18]

Pro-Carnivore Argument:

In the thousands of years dogs and humans have lived alongside one another, we've both evolved.

Today, dogs have genes that denote a neurological adaptation to cohabitation with humans. Some of these genes are key in the brain function and nervous system development related to the behavioral changes central to dog domestication.

The point?

It's not surprising to find that genes between the dog and wolf vary. After 10,000+ years, it's to be expected.

The pro-carnivore side argues[19] that a difference in ten genes would be considered an *adaptive* shift, and that it's not enough to alter the entire digestive evolution of a species.

Genetically speaking, dogs still share a near identical genetic makeup with wolves and other carnivorous candids. But as a bonus, they handle starch better.

Carnivore or omnivore – what do you think?

Don't worry. There are still some other areas we can look to for clarity. So let's keep digging.

Taxonomy May Tell an Accurate Story

Pro-Omnivore Argument:

The pro-omnivore side argues that it's not so black and white.

As we briefly touched upon earlier, the line between taxonomy classifications is not always clear-cut.

Within almost every category, there is a wide range of species and the different types of food on which they survive. Inside the Carnivora order, there are species surviving solely on prey animals, and species that consume both prey animals and plant matter.

In other words, there are always exceptions to the "rules."

Pro-Carnivore Argument:

A dog's taxonomic classification falls within the Carnivora order (meat eaters). They're in the same family as their wild relatives, gray wolves.

The pro-carnivore camp argues that dogs share a definitive number of biological and anatomical similarities with other carnivores. Just because dogs can stay *alive* on plant-based foods, that doesn't make them omnivores.

There's probably more insightful information to guide us than simple taxonomy classifications, but there's no denying the validity of a classification system scientists have used for hundreds of years.

Comparative Anatomy is Also Convincing:

While there are stark differences between herbivores and carnivores, the omnivore and carnivore share more in common.

Anatomical Tools

Pro Omnivore Argument:

As the omnivore camp points out, *both* omnivores and carnivores have sharp claws and powerful bodies. If an animal eats meat (regardless of the amount) they must have the equipment needed to hunt and kill.

Based on these factors alone, there's nothing within this category that *clearly* labels one animal a carnivore and the other an omnivore.

Jaw Structure & Teeth

When it comes to the structure and mobility of the jaw, the differences between carnivores and herbivores are well defined.

The omnivore is a bit trickier.

Some have a jaw structure closely resembling an herbivore's and others comparable to a carnivore.

For this reason, jaw structure alone isn't a defining factor. But would you like to know the key anatomical difference between these two classifications?

Teeth.

Pro Carnivore Argument:

Dogs do *not* possess dull, flat, square molars like animals built for consuming plants. A dog's molars are pointed and sharp.

Omnivores, on the other hand, have both sharp, pointed teeth in the front for latching on to prey, and flat molars in the back for grinding and crushing plant matter.

Even bears have these flat molars.

Bears are commonly used as examples in arguments claiming dogs as omnivores. But the teeth of dogs and bears differ significantly.

Based solely on the shape, dentition, and type of teeth, it seems as though a dog would fit the definition of a carnivore.

Saliva and The Enzyme Amylase

Pro-Carnivore Argument:

Amylase is an enzyme and it's something we humans have in our mouth, or within our saliva (hence the term: salivary amylase). This enzyme breaks complex carbohydrates into simple sugar.

It's simple. Dogs and cats do *not* come equipped with

salivary amylase.

Many people believe the absence of salivary amylase is an indicator dogs are *not* built to consume much plant matter. Why? They lack the enzyme to kick start carbohydrate digestion in the mouth.

Pro-carnivore theorists maintain that just because dogs can adapt to a starch-based diet, that doesn't mean it's a biologically appropriate source of nourishment.

Pro-Omnivore Argument:

It's true; dogs don't produce the enzyme amylase in their saliva. But they do produce it later in the body, within the pancreas. For this reason, those who believe dogs are omnivores don't consider the lack of *salivary* amylase an important clue here.

They also consider the fact that dogs have been shown to adapt by producing more amylase over time as an indicator they belong in the omnivore grouping.

GI Tract Format & Function

Can the shape, size, length or girth of an animal's GI tract provide insight into what they were meant to eat?

Some people believe so.

Pro-Carnivore Argument:

This group strongly believes the stomach and intestines of the domestic dog imply a carnivorous predisposition.

To start, dogs come equipped with digestive tracts built for consuming meat that aligns with other carnivores – short, simple, smooth and highly acidic.

In fact, a dog's digestive tract averages about 2 feet in length. Compare that to humans, where the digestive tract averages about 30 feet.

While GI tract length alone may not be a defining factor, other pro-carnivore theorists claim it's not about intestinal length.

Some suggest that when comparing an animal's GI tract, we should ignore length, girth or volume. What's most appropriate according to this theory is the "coefficient of fermentation."

In a nutshell, herbivores are capable of extracting nutrition from plant matter because they ferment it.

This = high coefficient of fermentation.

Carnivores aren't equipped for this and don't easily extract nutrients from plant material.

This = low coefficient of fermentation.

Pro-Omnivore Argument:

Supporters of the omnivore theory don't consider the length or width of an animal's GI tract as an accurate gauge.

While the GI tracts of many omnivores tend to fall in the middle ranges, it's worth noting that certain omnivorous animals like bears for instance, may have a GI set up similar to a carnivore.

It's also hard to prove. We're simply reading estimations and observances.

This information is not easily verifiable. And there's no library or encyclopedia that lists the size, length, girth or volume of a GI tract by animal.

Plus, there's no standard when it comes to measurements associated with the GI Tract that clearly labels an animal as a true carnivore or omnivore.

Animal Behavior

A dog's instinctual behaviors may provide clues into how they should be classified.

Pro-Carnivore Argument:

This group claims dog's innate behaviors are carnivorous.

One common behavior: digging. Similar to wolves, dogs have a tendency to dig to hide things, just as wolves dig to hide parts of meals for future snacking.

Dogs are also predatory by nature.

Pups and young animals play fight, wrestle, roll around and bite one another's necks. This doesn't happen by chance, it's *practice*.

A drive to chase prey is the reason dogs instinctively go after things that run. We also shouldn't forget that dogs were bred and used as hunters throughout history.

Pro-Omnivore Argument:

The pro-omnivore camp tends to dismiss these arguments, stating that omnivores also take part in these behaviors, so they are not exclusively carnivorous.

In addition, they argue dogs lost much of their wildness due to domestication, and no longer hunt for their food. Instead, their caregivers feed them.

Studying the Wolf's Diet Provides More Clues

Pro-Omnivore Argument:

Wolves also ate plants and grains, according to wolf researchers. Not only did wolves indulge in berries, fruits or grasses in the wild, but they also ate the grains and plant matter contained in their prey's stomach.

The following quotes from various scientists, researches and authors acknowledge this:

- In "The Diet of Feral Carnivores: a Review of Stomach Content Analysis"[20] both Landry and Van Ruining state: *"The staple diet of carnivores living in a natural setting includes other animals, carrion, and **occasionally fruits and grasses"***

- And from Dogs: A Startling New Understanding of Canine Origin, Behavior & Evolution by Coppinger R, Coppinger L,[21] the following is said: *"Scraps of meat, bones, pieces of carcass, **rotten greens and fruit**, fish guts, **discarded seed and grains**, animals guts and head..."*

- In "What a Wolf Eats: Research on Wild Candids can Help Inform Dietary Planning for Dogs,"[22] Puotinen can be found saying: *"Their preference is freshly killed meat, **but when that's not available, they'll eat anything that could remotely be considered edible"***

What's more, David L. Mech, American wolf expert and senior research scientist for the U.S. Department of the Interior's U.S. Geological Survey shares similar findings. In his book "Wolves: Behavior, Ecology, and Conservation[23]," he notes:

- "Because of the greater availability of fruit, wolves in the southern portions of Eurasia **may feed on plant material more extensively"**

• **"Fruit may provide vitamins for wolves"**

• "It also feeds on all the other animals in its environment, scavenges, and **can even eat fruits and berries**"

• "Because **wolves may consume fruits such as berries**, sweet taste receptors would be adaptive..."

Pro-Carnivore Argument:

This group understands the research and agrees that wolves may choose to supplement with a *small* amount of plant matter. But they stress, it's not a large part of their diet.

As such, they encourage their opponents to review the language used by researchers. More often than not, it implies the amount of plant material in the wolf's diet is small.

Additionally, they stress that the definition of a carnivore is an animal that consumes a diet "consisting *mainly* of or *exclusively* of animal tissue." The fact that wolves prefer meat and that meat is the main part of their diet implies they are carnivores.

What's more, they point out statements made by Mech in the same book that claim wolves tend to leave stomach contents behind after a kill[24]. This contradicts many pro-omnivore claims.

According to Mech's research, wolves tear into the body cavity of large prey to consume internal organs like the lungs, heart, and liver. The stomach is usually punctured in the process, spilling the contents. While wolves typically consume the stomach wall and intestinal lining of their prey, "vegetation within the stomach or intestines is of no interest to them."

With anything, I'm sure this depends on the animal, the

location, and the availability of food. Does this mean wolves never ate the stomach contents of a prey animal?

No.

It suggests that in the big picture, it appears it's not a regular practice for these animals.

Let's Define Plant Matter

As you can see, the consumption of plant material in the wolf's diet is a hot topic, as it's often used to support the use of carbohydrates in the dog's diet today.

However, this is not an apples-to-apples argument.

Wolves aren't eating starchy or cellulose-rich foods like potatoes, peas, corn and grains in the wild.

Wolves have been observed eating items like grasses, wild herbs, tree bark, and so on.

Even if plant matter was more than a small part of the diet, the carbohydrates we feed dogs today are drastically different than the plant material most omnivores consume in the wild.

The same goes for fruit. Historically, wolves have had access to low-starch fruits like seasonal berries. They weren't eating bananas or plantains.

In short, not all carbohydrates are created equal.

Does Personal Preference Count for Anything?

Pro-Omnivore Argument

Many of you may be thinking: "Wait a minute... My dog loves broccoli, pineapple, carrots, etc."

Some dogs *love* fruits and veggies.

But any dog owner can agree: dogs don't approach plant material in the same way they approach meat.

Pro-Carnivore Argument:

The palate of the average dog tells us: Dogs have an *undeniable* preference for meat.

If you've ever given your dog meat scraps, or even meat-based treats, it's usually devoured in the blink of an eye.

Yet, when tossed a vegetable or piece of fruit, most dogs seem confused, uncertain, or appear awkward eating it.

This is not peer-reviewed science, but it's worth considering.

Carnivore or Omnivore: Can a Dog Fit in the Middle?

Many people believe so. In fact, there are two major types of carnivores[25]: obligate and facultative.

Obligate carnivores are strict carnivores. They must have meat as the main component of their diet and they need it to *thrive*. Nature designed their bodies to derive energy and nutrient requirements through animal meat, tissue, bones and organs alone.

Facultative carnivores are more flexible.

They share similar anatomical, biological and physical characteristics with obligate carnivores. They consume a diet of animal meat, tissue, bones and organs to obtain energy and nutrient requirements.

But while they *prefer* meat, the facultative carnivore can survive on whatever is available.

This is confirmed by both the *behavior* and the *diet* of wild dogs. They have a greater knack for scavenging than other obligate carnivores, like cats for example. Plus, dogs are willing to eat non-animal foods like berries, fruits, and grasses.

The facultative carnivore is commonly viewed as "a carnivore with omnivore tendencies."

Pro-Omnivore Argument:

Pro-omnivores acknowledge obligate carnivores have a greater nutritional need for meat, and may not tolerate non-meat based foods as well.

But they point out that while some obligate carnivores (like snakes) may die on a carbohydrate diet, other animals (like domestic cats) can survive on non-biologically appropriate foods.

They also assert that facultative carnivores are so close in functional behavior to omnivores, they're hardly distinguishable.

Pro-Carnivore Argument:

This group believes dogs are, without a doubt, facultative carnivores.

While there is no clearly defined ratio when it comes to plant and animal material that can distinguish carnivores and omnivores apart, the fact that dogs share more similarities with carnivores is evidence enough.

Plus, they argue that just because an animal can *survive* on biologically inappropriate foods does not mean they will *thrive* on those foods or reach optimal health.

This group opts to feed foods that animals are built for and foods that animals show a clear preference for.

So, Is the Dog a Carnivore or an Omnivore?

This is a tough question to answer.

There's no definitive line separating precisely where a carnivore ends and where an omnivore begins. There will always be room for individual interpretation.

There's more at stake here than scientific pursuit or personal viewpoint. Thousands of businesses (mostly the pet food industry) are based on the information touted by either side.

If a clear winner emerges, the other side has a lot to lose.

Moving Forward

When it comes to nutrition, there are a lot of unknowns.

The goal of this chapter was not to confuse you further, but to provide you with an objective presentation of all the facts.

From here, you must come to your own conclusion.

The components of a canine ancestral diet are important and worth discussing, but don't get too *hung up* on them.

What's most important is feeding your dog a diet that will grow, heal, and nourish their bodies.

It's time to learn more about pet food, where it began, and what it's like today.

Key Takeaway:

There may never be 100% agreement on whether the dog is a carnivore or omnivore but a majority of the research supports the idea that dogs are facultative carnivores.

PART
The History of Dog Food
THREE

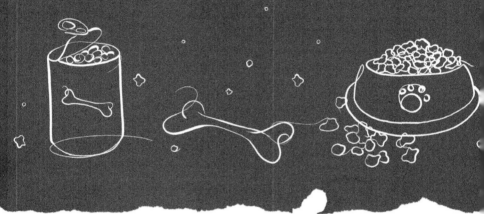

"Many a small thing has been made large by the right kind of advertising"

-Mark Twain

At this point, we know more about the domestic dog and their ancestors than most pet parents. But there's still one thing most dog owners don't know about...

A life *without* dog food.

Every single one of us grew up with the concept of dog food. In fact, we all came to age in a time when dog food reigned supreme.

This means most of us don't know:

- What dogs ate before dog food existed
- How dog food got its start
- When dog food came to replace real food

Roll up the shades and let some light in. After today, you'll no longer be in the dark about the history of dog food.

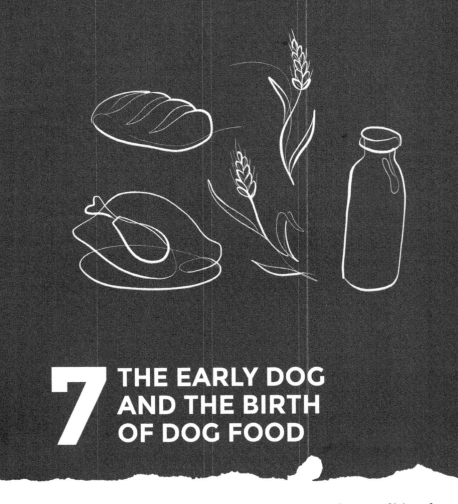

7 THE EARLY DOG AND THE BIRTH OF DOG FOOD

It's safe to say a vast majority of dog owners buy traditional wet or dry pet food for their dogs.

Here's what's crazy:

Few dog owners ever even question the safety or nutritional value, let alone if there's a better option.

The concept of "dog food" is ingrained in us.

It's all we know. Dog food has existed longer than we've been alive. In fact, there isn't a *single* person alive today that grew up in a time when dog food wasn't the norm.

But it wasn't always the age of dog food.

Let's learn how dog food was born.

The Dog Food Timeline

Dog food is a mere speck in canine history.

Let's assume dogs were domesticated 10,000 years ago (according to some research, it's much longer). Dog food was first conceptualized in the 1800s.

Dog food has existed for only 155 years. The time period before dog food?

8140 B.C. until the year 1859.

That's a massive amount of time, and it's worth exploring.

So what did dogs eat *after* they were domesticated, but *before* pet food was invented?

Dinner for The Early Domestic Dog

As you may remember, early dogs were specialized and domesticated to work. So how did these working machines fuel their bodies?

The answer is REAL FOOD.

According to statements from historical literature, early domestic dogs were fed scraps or ate what they could hunt and catch for themselves.

What were scraps exactly?

That depended on the time period, location and income level of the dog owner. Written accounts suggest scraps likely included:

• Raw meat trimmings

- Fat
- Organs (hearts, livers, lungs)
- Bones
- By-products and other body parts (hooves, poultry feet, etc.)
- Vegetables (potatoes, cabbage, and the like)
- Milk
- Eggs
- Grains and Breads

Where did they come from?

Leftovers from a meal, surplus from an individual's hunting quarry, or even scraps from the local butcher.

Social Status, Wealth, and the Early Canine Diet

The same rules that apply today also applied back then. Income level directly correlated with quality of diet.

Dogs of the rich ate far *better* than dogs of the poor.

Dogs of common folk were likely fed meager diets of what could be spared. This may have included:

- Bones, bread, potatoes, cabbage
- Bread soaked in milk and bones from dead animals
- Anything else the dog managed to scrounge

It was a different story for dogs of the wealthy. These animals were fed top-notch diets.

During the Middle Ages, European royalty hired kennel cooks to feed their hounds large batches of stew made from grains, vegetables, meat scraps, or meat by-products like hearts, livers, and lungs of various livestock.

Some people even made a living by searching the streets for dead horses to cut up and sell to rich dog owners.

The rich and royal fed their dogs a diet superior to what most ordinary people ate.

This included proteins like roast duck and other expensive cuts of meat. Empress Tzu Hsi of China was known to provide her dog with delicacies like shark fins, quail breast, and antelope milk.

Notice a Food Quality Trend?

Back in the day, elite canine diets were *meat-based* diets.

But meat-heavy diets were generally only affordable for the wealthy. Less privileged dog owners fed what they had. This usually included more grains, breads, vegetable scraps, and bones.

This sounds similar to the dog food landscape today:

You get what you pay for.

Early Dog Owners Possessed a Wealth of Knowledge

Early dog owners understood dogs were natural protein-processing machines.

They observed these animals in their natural element and witnessed what they hunted or scavenged.

It's conceivable early dog owners knew far more about dogs than the average dog owner does now. Not only did they train and employ dogs for a variety of jobs, but they were instrumental in creating the breeds we have today.

I think it's safe to say they were well aware of a dog's dietary needs.

So when did things shift?

The Shift in the Way We Feed Our Dogs

In the mid-eighteenth century, society began to change.

The industrial revolution was upon us. Amidst the pollution, smog and billowing smoke emerged something new:

A growing middle class.

With it came an increase in discretionary income and more leisure time. Dogs dwindled as working members of society and were regarded as luxury items, or "pets."

Dogs no longer fended for themselves. Instead, their caregivers fed them.

As people became more specialized and less self-sufficient, they started visiting grocers and butcher shops instead of growing and harvesting their own food.

So how did families feed their pets affordably?

At this point in time, the idea of excess (especially in regards to food) was a relatively new concept. While times were changing, most people were not swimming in leftovers.

Regardless, these societal advancements gave birth to an idea that had no basis in fact whatsoever.

This idea sprouted like a seed, propagating through the masses:

Dogs must be *civilized.*

Wild dogs ate raw meat, but domesticated dogs shouldn't.

This naive concept has plagued the population ever since and paved the way for the birth of the pet food industry.

The Original Dog Food

In 1859, James Spratt had the perfect solution.

Spratt was a young electrician from Ohio with an entrepreneurial spirit that couldn't be denied.

On a voyage to London, Spratt spotted crewmembers throwing leftover hardtack along the docks. He paid particular attention to the pack of dogs scavenging the dockyards, enthusiastically devouring every last piece.

What is hardtack?

Early processed food.

The military ate it on long voyages in the absence of real, perishable food. It had a cracker or biscuit-like consistency with a long shelf life.

That's when Spratt had his grand idea: selling cheap, easy-to-serve biscuits to the growing population of urban dog owners.

His creation was coined "Spratt's Meat Fibrine Dog Cakes." These early baked goods were made with wheat, beetroot, and vegetables, with beef blood binding the concoction together.

The rest, as they say, was history.

Pet Food Advertising Was Born

Spratt's Fibrine Dog Cakes first came onto the scene in England in 1860.

They were a huge success, allowing Spratt to take the business to New York ten years later.

His new idea took off with lightning speed thanks to his clever marketing strategy:

He held dog shows to market his treats.

Boom.

Just like that, Spratt's was a hit.

Spratt's not only spawned the birth of dog food and encouraged other companies to follow suit, but his promotional strategy sparked the birth of pet food advertising.

Why Are We Talking About Advertising?

This is a raw feeding book. Why should you care about pet food advertising?

Let me put it simply.

Advertising is *everything*.

It's everywhere. It influences every decision you make – consciously or subconsciously (we call the later hypnosis).

To understand how we got where we are today, we must understand where things began.

Pet food advertising was the catalyst.

Key Takeaway:
Before dog food existed, dogs ate meat-based diets made from REAL FOOD.

8 WELCOME TO THE AGE OF PET FOOD ADVERTISING

The impact of advertising is rooted much deeper than most people are aware. Many of things we've known our entire life or the traditions we follow without question began with an advertising campaign.

Believe it or not, this is exactly what happened with dog food.

Real Life Advertising Example

Let's start with a fairy tale every young girl grows up hearing.

It's not Cinderella or Sleeping Beauty. It's the engagement story. You know, when two individuals fall madly in love and decide to spend the rest of their lives together.

One partner gets down on one knee and asks for the other's hand in marriage. They then shell out thousands of dollars for a diamond engagement ring to make it official.

How did that tradition begin?

With the most epic ad campaign of all time.

Diamond rings aren't a timeless symbol of love or an ancient tradition, but a strategic marketing ploy by the DeBeers Corporation. Before the 1930s, no one exchanged rings. They simply popped the age-old question.

That is, until DeBeers launched their massive ad campaign.

The message?

They claimed the only way for a real man to show his love was with an expensive diamond.

The public ate it up.

Every element of the traditional American engagement was designed to make a profit for DeBeers. Where did the "two months salary" standard come from?

The ad campaign. It was an arbitrary number decided by marketing executives.

What's impressive about this campaign is that diamonds are intrinsically worthless. Don't believe me? The DeBeers Chairman was quoted saying exactly this in 1999[26].

DeBeers runs a global monopoly on these hunks of crystalized carbon. They buy all the diamonds, restrict supply, and jack up rates.

That's the beauty in the success of this campaign.

A century of advertising has *embedded* the idea so deeply in our culture that knowing this information doesn't change a thing. It doesn't change public perception or action.

That's the power of advertising.

Not surprisingly, dog food followed a similar story.

The Father of Pet Food Advertising

James Spratt[27] is well known for being first to market with his dog biscuits. What's often overlooked is his role in creating pet food advertisements.

Spratt was a savvy businessman and a marketing genius. He single-handedly spawned the billion-dollar pet food industry and the substantial advertising market that now accompanies it.

As we learned, Spratt first hooked the public and gained visibility for his products through dog shows. After the wild success of this marketing tactic, Spratt continued to target participants and spectators at various events.

In 1876, he used the Centennial Exhibition (the first official world fair in the US) as a promotional opportunity by providing free food to exhibitors.

He was also the first to construct a billboard in London, and bought the front cover to the first journal of the American Kennel Club to broadcast his brand.

Why was he so massively successful?

Aside from being a relentless advertiser, he appealed to

emotion and ego. He promoted his products through snob appeal. Spratt convinced Americans who fed table scraps to their dogs to buy products they didn't *need.*

His company even targeted health-conscious dog owners, pioneering the concept of animal life stages and appropriate foods for each stage.

He was the godfather of pet food advertising.

Following in Spratt's Footsteps

After the success of Spratt's Meat Fibrine Dog Cakes, other companies followed suit:

• A veterinarian introduced A.C. Daniel's Medicated Dog Bread in the 1880s.

• The F.H. Bennett Company opened their doors in the early 1900s. They were the first company to produce dog biscuits shaped as bones. They also conceptualized puppy food and packaged kibble in various sizes for different dog breeds.

• Ken-L Ration was the first company to can dog food in the US. It was made from horsemeat and was wildly popular. Bitten by the advertising bug, the company supported events and sponsored a popular radio show: "The Adventures of Rin Tin Tin."

• Nabisco eventually bought Bennett's company and rebranded to Milk-Bones. The company campaigned vigorously. They wanted Milk Bones to be the standard in dog food. With an army of 3,000 salesmen, they put product on every food store shelf in the country.

The pet food business was flourishing.

Canned food continued to gain more and more traction. It eventually outperformed kibble in popularity as dog owners noticed their dogs preferred wet food to dry.

Wet food reigned supreme for a few years, until something big sparked major changes.

The Great Depression, World War II, and Dog Food

As the economy collapsed and the average American family fell into hardship, pet food companies had another stroke of advertising genius.

They appealed to our pocketbooks.

Dog food companies began to market their products as more affordable alternatives to providing food at home. This fostered more competition among pet food brands for consumer dollars. Advertising messages grew bolder.

Consumers were overwhelmed with the message that raw meat was too expensive and created fussy, picky eaters.

As for the people who still believed *fresh* foods were ideal, advertising convinced them their dogs could do particularly well on pet food. More importantly, the purchase would save the family money.

In the midst of World War II, the government started rationing tin and meat. This made canning difficult and expensive. Eventually, wet pet food dominance hit a sharp decline.

Dry food became popular again, and soon took center stage.

The Fallacy That Real Food Was Harmful

Right from the start, pet food manufacturers discouraged customers from feeding or supplementing their dog's diet with anything but food from a box.

A culture of dependence was being forged right under our

noses.

As time went on, these marketing messages only grew stronger. An early, lucrative campaign pushed the idea that real food (or "people food") was harmful.

This concept was vital in propelling the dog food industry forward.

How?

Enter lobbying.

The Pet Food Institute was created. They were a lobbying group for the now-enormous pet food industry.

In 1964, they began the mother of all campaigns with the goal of getting people to stop feeding their dogs *anything* but packaged dog food.

Propaganda soon bombarded consumers.

The Pet Food Institute funded reports appearing in magazines detailing the benefits of processed foods. They even produced a radio segment about the "dangers of table scraps."

Commercials ensued, and competing brands found themselves in "quality wars."

Pet food companies squabbled over who had the purest beef. One company even recruited *Bonanza* star Lorne Greene to feature in an Alpo commercial.

Over time, advertising messages became more far-fetched and flat out inaccurate. Soon, dog food advertisers claimed dog food was *required* for good health, and was actually better for our beloved pets.

Table scraps and real food became *harmful*; despite being successfully fed for thousands of years.

Pet food advertisers used fear, uncertainty and doubt to convince dog owners to feed processed junk. At this point (over fifty years ago), the dog food industry spent an incredible $50 million a year on advertising.

This strategic effort set the stage for the beliefs on dog food today.

Processed pet food eventually replaced table scraps as the most popular way to feed America's booming dog population.

The Age of Veterinary Endorsements

By this point, veterinary medicine was well established.

Before veterinary medicine, people cared for dogs on their own. They may have reached out to others with more experience, but official or licensed "animal doctors" did not exist.

As pets grew in popularity, this gave rise to self-proclaimed experts. Many of which gave advice on canine diets, dog behavior, and the like.

Because of the dominant thought during this period that dogs needed to be civilized, a strong preference toward cooked meat and processed dog food was brewing in our culture.

Eventually, demand grew, and veterinary medicine was officially founded in the United States in 1895, thirty-five years *after* pet food.

Why is this significant?

Veterinary medicine was founded during a period of early growth and expansion in the world.

It was a time when people thought *convenience* was progress. Only wild dogs ate raw meat. Domestic dogs were "civilized" and ate special food from the grocery store.

Veterinary medicine was born in a time when pet food was king.

In other words, the entire veterinary industry was founded on the coat tails of the pet food industry.

It only took us over a hundred years to realize *convenience* isn't progress. Processed, chemically laden foods are doing more harm than good, and Mother Nature has been right all along.

Fresh, organic, real foods are best.

Influencer Marketing Takes Hold

Veterinary medicine couldn't have been founded at a more perfect time.

The love, affection, and attachment for furry family members continued to tug at America's heartstrings.

More and more money was spewed into the pet food industry each day, and business was thriving. At the same time, the competitive landscape of the pet food industry was heating up.

During this time, all the brands were claiming their products, ingredients, and formulas were superior. Eventually, the messaging became stale and lost impact.

As the television show Survivor so brilliantly puts it, marketers needed to "outwit, outplay, and outlast" the competition.

Say hello to influencer marketing: the practice of identifying and targeting individuals with influence over potential buyers.

How did big pet food do it?

They utilized veterinarians for endorsements.

After all, it must be true if it comes from a vet, right?

That was the sentiment of the general population at the time. Anything from a veterinarian's mouth was accepted as a universal truth.

Understandably so.

But our history is riddled with examples of advertising messages and influential figures being "bought."

Do you know cigarettes were once "physician tested and approved?

From the 1930s to the 1950s, doctors lit up the pages of cigarette advertisements. They weren't alone. Dentists, celebrities, babies, and even Santa Claus touted their approval for big tobacco as well.

This was advertising in America, a sort of subtle brainwashing.

"Complete and Balanced Nutrition" Propaganda

Big pet food was booming. The majority of dog owners were content, blindly following the advice from so-called experts and buying into every word vocalized from the pet food industry.

Yet some pet parents remained skeptical.

Armed to combat skeptics, the pet food industry set their targets on consumers who hadn't fully adopted pet food.

They piggybacked off the idea that the traditional canine diets – real food - were somehow incomplete. What followed is a concept that is still with us today, over a hundred years later.

The message:

Dog food was *"complete and balanced"* nutrition.

Homemade diets, on the other hand, were inadequate, deficient of important nutrients, and lacking balance.

Factories kicked into gear.

Almost overnight, pet food packaging was labeled as "complete and balanced nutrition." With this campaign, the pet food industry was able to convince pet owners that no additional supplementation was needed in a dog's diet.

Soon, vets advised that meat-based diets were incomplete nutrition, that dog food needed to be fortified with vitamins and minerals (as if real food wasn't already nutrient-dense), carbohydrates were necessary, and too much protein could be harmful

The Modern Pet Food Landscape

Over the years, pet food prospered and further "advancements" in dog food were announced.

These so-called advancements were merely clever ad campaigns disguised as groundbreaking pet food formulas and new product lines.

And they were wildly successful.

Brands continued to advertise, create new products, and grow their reach. Soon, we had specialty diets for certain diseases and health conditions, except the ingredients weren't much different. In fact, not much changed other than the packaging and marketing.

What propelled it forward?

Influence.

These product lines received an air of credibility because they were *only* available in veterinary offices.

Another brainchild in pet food was the concept of "premium dog food." With the promise of higher quality ingredients and seductive packaging, this inflated the value of the product.

Brands further expanded product lines into diets formulated for puppies and senior dogs. After that came diets for performance and maintenance.

Consumers became overwhelmed with options. Many thought they were already feeding optimum nutrition. Now they had to feed the premium lines if they wanted the best for their dogs.

Big pet food continued to grow and utilize brilliant marketing schemes. Next came capitalizing on health movements.

Just as dog food has progressed over the years, so has society. We've grown leaps and bounds in the health department.

Today, we recognize convenience foods often lack proper nutrition. Trends of getting back to our roots and consuming fresh, organic foods are becoming the dominant thought again.

As the American public's perception of health shifted, dog owners began to question conventional wisdom and challenge the pet food industry. They pushed for more nutritious and appropriate food for dogs.

What did the pet food industry do?

They responded to demand with new products and fresh, shiny marketing campaigns.

Consumers soon saw grain-free food and all-natural product lines and brands (hint: these aren't much better).

Packaging featured pictures of wolves. Labels claimed recipes contained more meat. Slogans reminded us that diets were formulated based on a dog's ancestors.

Fortunately, we have more options today.

But we still need to look past seductive packaging and advertising claims. Because at the end of the day, there's nothing ancestral about dry, crusty pellets being poured out of a paper bag.

The Raw Revolution

Raw feeding isn't a trend.

It occurs in Mother Nature each and every day.

People have been feeding raw diets for ages. And many experienced dog owners continued to feed in this manner, even during the age of pet food.

Raw diets aren't new.

What's new is the awareness of a better way.

There's more information out there on the merits of a raw diet than ever before. This feeding style is gaining traction and popularity among dog owners fed up with crap food and sick, ailing dogs.

The exciting part?

Commercial raw food companies have emerged, and today we have a living, breathing, and growing raw pet food industry.

Ready to challenge the status quo?

Pet Food Advertising Summed up

A hundred and fifty years since its genesis, pet food has

grown to a multi billion-dollar industry, and is the fastest growing sector in all of the food industry.

Did you know that most grocery stores in the U.S. devote more shelf space to canned and kibbled dog food than they do baby food or breakfast cereal?

The pet food industry accomplished the unthinkable.

Big pet food instilled the idea of convenience and frugality in our pet's nutrition. Consumers were left out of canine nutrition, *on purpose*. It was portrayed as a highly complex issue meant for veterinarians and dog food companies.

Dog owners stopped using their heads and put their trust in pet food companies as the authority on canine nutrition.

Consequently, there's been a correlation between the rise of processed pet food and the declining health of the domestic dog for quite some time now.

Skin issues, allergies, reoccurring infections, diabetes, and cancer are just a few of the conditions the average dog has to look forward to these days.

But here's what you really need to know:

What the heck is in your pet's food?

Key Takeaway:

Well-crafted advertising campaigns persuaded public opinion that REAL FOOD (i.e table scraps) were dangerous and incomplete.

PART

What's Wrong With Traditonally Prepared Dog Food?

FOUR

"The food your dog eats can be the safest form of medicine or the slowest form of poison"

-Ann Wigmore

You and I both know:

Dog food is not all it's cracked up to be.

It's why you're reading this book. Deep down, you must have some lingering *doubt* about dog food.

Perhaps a friend or family member steered you in this direction. Maybe a stranger made a comment you couldn't shake. That, or you landed here through your own quest for knowledge.

Either way, you're set on answers to this burning question:

What's wrong with dog food?

I'm not going to sugar coat it. There's a lot of ground to cover.

But to simplify, I've grouped my grievances into three main categories:

1. Dog food ingredients are not always biologically appropriate.

2. Dog food ingredients are often low quality and potentially toxic.

3. Dog food is heavily processed and laden with chemicals.

Let's dive in.

DOG FOOD INGREDIENTS

9 ARE NOT ALWAYS BIOLOGICALLY APPROPRIATE

"Ancestral" tends to be a word thrown around loosely by pet food companies. Add some protein in the formula and a wolf on the package and we're good to go, right?

Not exactly.

If you're looking to understand why traditional dog food ingredients are less than ideal, pay close attention to this chapter.

I'm going to show you exactly what's wrong with many of the biologically *inappropriate* items in today's dog food products.

Let's Start With Macronutrients

We'd need to create a series of encyclopedias to cover the hundreds of ingredients in individual brands of dog food.

But who wants to read that?

Instead, we'll cover only what you need to know to make better decisions about what to feed your dog.

We'll start by breaking ingredients into major macronutrient categories:

- Protein
- Carbohydrates
- Fat

The Lowdown on Protein

My first quarrel with pet food is about the protein. Here are the primary complaints:

1. Type of protein
2. Quantity of protein

Type of Protein: Animal Protein vs. Plant Protein

By now, you understand protein is the main component of a canine ancestral diet. To be specific: animal protein.

Here's the problem:

Many pet foods also include plant-based protein because it's cheaper.

But as facultative carnivores, dogs are best equipped to digest and process animal proteins.

Let me explain why.

Animal protein is a *complete* protein for dogs. It contains all the essential amino acids dogs need to thrive.

In case you need a refresher, amino acids are the building blocks of protein. Dogs need 22 amino acids to be healthy. But their bodies can only make 12 of those 22. The remaining 10 must come from the foods they eat, which is why they're called *essential* amino acids.

The protein found in animal tissue has a complete amino acid profile. Plant proteins on the other hand are incomplete. They lack the correct proportions of amino acids for dogs.

While some species (like humans) have the physiological ability to turn plant proteins into a complete amino acid profile, dogs cannot.

Knowing this, manufacturers often add amino acids back to their foods to make up for the cheaper, biologically inappropriate sources of protein in their formulas.

Without this step, they risk amino acid deficiencies in their four-legged customers. But these additions are usually synthetic (i.e. fake) meaning they were made in a lab and don't come from real food.

Whatever you believe dogs should be eating, one thing cannot be denied:

Dogs have an *instinctual* preference toward animal flesh.

So you may agree that meat should be the main ingredient and foundation to a healthy canine diet.

This leads me to the next beef (so to speak).

Protein Quantity: What Traditional Pet Foods Lacks

How much animal protein is in dog food?

Meat should be the main ingredient in dog food. Many times, it's not. Dog food contains all kind of other cheap and affordable fillers to drive costs down.

Why? Meat is expensive.

As a consumer, you have no idea *how much* animal protein is in the dog food you purchase.

Most dog food companies make little effort to disclose the amount of meat in a product. The only way to get a reasonable idea is to read the ingredient list.

All ingredients must be listed in descending order according to their preprocessing weights. At what position is meat listed? More often than not, it's further down the list.

What if it's listed first?

Good news. Unfortunately, you still can't trust it.

Why?

Pet food manufacturer use loopholes.

They realize consumers have become more interested in pet food ingredients. They also know you want to see meat listed as the first ingredient.

Here's what's slick:

The meat at the top of the ingredient label was probably weighed *before* it was dehydrated. Before dehydration, meat is about 70% water and heavy, which is why it made its way to the top of the list.

But once it's dehydrated (and *all* meat in pet food is), it ends up being the 2nd, 3rd, 4th, or 5th ingredient in that list.

If that doesn't work, pet food manufacturers have a more

deceptive tactic they can use.

Ingredient splitting.

This practice is exactly as it sounds. You divide more abundant, yet inferior, ingredients into smaller portions.

Pet food manufacturers use ingredient splitting to *artificially* raise meat to a higher position on the ingredient label. And they do this while simultaneously *lowering* an inferior ingredient.

How does it work?

Let's say you're looking at a bag of dog food labeled, "Chicken and Rice." What you may not realize is the rice was separated into different ingredients: brown rice, rice flour and rice bran.

This allows pet food manufacturers to divide the weight of the rice by three. Now, meat jumps to the top of the ingredient list when in reality rice outnumbers the chicken 3:1.

Thanks to the folks that regulate the sale of pet foods, this bag of dog food can now be labeled "Chicken and Rice." But a more truthful name would be "rice and a little bit of chicken."

Watch out for this with other ingredients besides rice:

- Corn (corn gluten meal, corn flour, whole ground corn)
- Peas (peas, pea protein, pea flour)
- Potatoes (dried potatoes, potato starch, potato flour, potato protein)

The moral of the protein story:

Dogs are built to thrive on meat-based diets.

But most dog food contains *little* meat and tons of

carbohydrates. Statistically speaking, dogs that consume carbohydrate-heavy diets tend to have poor nutrition and experience more health issues.

The Carbohydrate Conundrum

My second dispute with dog food centers on carbohydrates.

Just like protein, the problem lies in:

1. Quantity of carbohydrates
2. Type of carbohydrates included.

But first...

Are Carbohydrates Required For Good Canine Health?

The answer might surprise you.

According to experts, carbohydrates are *not* required to sustain life in dogs.

These experts include The National Research Council (NRC) and The Association of American Feed Control Officials (AAFCO). The later regulates the sale and distribution of animal feeds.

In a 2006 committee on Animal Nutrition, the NRC confirmed dogs have no nutritional requirements for carbohydrates[28]. And in their 2010 Pet Food Nutrient Profiles[29], the AAFCO concluded carbohydrates are not essential to a healthy canine diet.

Leading veterinary textbooks agree as well.

Canine and Feline Nutrition[30], co authored by scientists from Iams state:

> *"The fact that dogs and cats do not require carbohydrates is immaterial because the nutrient content of most*

commercial foods includes (carbohydrates)."

Small Animal Clinical Nutrition[31], IV, published by the founder of Science Diet states:

> *"Dogs and cats do not have an absolute dietary requirement for carbohydrates in the same way that essential amnio acids or fatty acids must be provided... From a practical sense, the answer of this question is of little importance because there are carbohydrates in most food ingredients used in commercially prepared dog foods."*

And The Waltham Book of Companion Animal Nutrition[32] says:

> *"There is no known minimum dietary requirement for carbohydrate..."*

Now, let's find out where dog food went wrong with carbohydrates.

Carbohydrates in Pet Food: The Quantity is Too High

At this point, we understand the natural diet of dogs contained almost no carbohydrates.

Today, dogs are ingesting wheat, corn, rice, potatoes and a range of other carbohydrate-heavy foods. In fact, carbs represent a dominant proportion is most dry dog foods, estimated at a whopping 46-74%.

Compare this to a canine ancestral diet, which might contain 0-15% carbohydrates, and you'll notice dogs today are experiencing carb *overload*.

If Carbohydrates Are Not Ancestral Food Items, Why Include Them?

If dogs didn't eat these foods in the wild, why are they eating them today?

Great question.

Pet food manufacturers want us to believe pet food should be convenient and more affordable than "people food."

Carbs are cheap filler foods.

They're abundant, maintain a long shelf life, and are essential components of kibble. What's troubling is none of the reasons listed above have anything to do with nutrition.

Carbohydrates in pet food exist to save money and increase profits.

What's more, carbohydrate-heavy pet food diets are linked to a host of health issues in dogs like: blood sugar fluctuations, obesity, insulin resistance, diabetes, and cancer, to name a few.

Yet veterinarians seem to offer little nutritional advice surrounding carbohydrates.

Here's what's even more ironic:

The conditions caused by excessive carbohydrate consumption in dogs are actually treated by prescribing processed pet food... that is, food that's super *high* carbohydrates.

Seems counterproductive, doesn't it?

Carbohydrate Types: The Good, The Bad & The Ugly

For the sake of thoroughness, let's analyze the types of carb-heavy ingredients found in pet food today:

• Grains
• Legumes
• Fruits & Vegetables

Evaluating The Grain

Today, dog food manufacturers use a wide variety of grains within their products. It's not uncommon to see wheat, corn, rice, oats, barley, rye, millets, and other types of grains.

But despite what pet food manufacturers claim, dogs do *not* have a biological need for carbohydrates, let alone grains.

Grains have a lackluster nutrient profile compared to fruits and vegetables. Plus, dogs have a hard time digesting them.

Here's what's important to know:

Grain-heavy diets promote insulin production. They also increase the production of inflammatory chemicals in the body. Insulin overproduction can cause problems with weight, contribute to obesity, or lead to diabetes.

Other grain-related problems can include:

• Allergies
• Food sensitivity
• Skin issues
• Yeast infections
• GI inflammation and upset
• An abundance of inflammatory chemicals in the body, leading to arthritis and cancer

It's also worth noting that grains are also high in starch and carry a high *glycemic index.*

These types of foods quickly turn into sugar when metabolized in your dog's body, which can lead to other unsightly problems like yeast and cancer formation.

Don't believe me? Here's what DVM, Dr. Karen Becker of Mercola Healthy Pets has to say about grains:

> *"As a holistic vet who is passionate about feeding pets species-appropriate nutrition, I'm frankly appalled at the number of veterinarians pushing grain-based dog food. All veterinarians are aware dogs have no biological requirement for starch... and all grains (and other carbs) break down into starch and ultimately, sugar."*

Grains Are Not an Ancestral Food Item

To see why grains have no place in dog food, let's consider grains in the wild.

I'm not going to tell you animals don't eat grains – that would be silly. But what many people don't realize is that many animals fed grains today, don't actually eat them in the wild.

Sure, some animals (like birds, rodents and some insects) have adapted to grain consumption. But for most animals, grain consumption is a *low* percentage of the diet, and doesn't usually occur year round.

Let's consider the cow.

Their natural diet consists of grass. Did they eat grains? Sure. They ate *whatever* was part of the grass. If we fast-forward to current day, you'll notice most cows are completely grain-fed.

The result? Cows are sick and unhealthy. They're pumped with antibiotics to fight off constant infections and other ailments.

Now consider grass-fed cows.

They tend to be healthier, produce meat with a better nutritional profile, and require fewer antibiotics to stay healthy[33].

If grain-heavy diets aren't the best fit for cows, why are they a good fit for a domesticated wolf?

Dr. Karen Becker, DVM echoes this concern[34]:

> *"It's also common knowledge that the natural diets of canines contain almost no carbs, with the primary source being predigested grasses, fruits and veggies found in the stomachs of prey animals. Dogs have short digestive tracts and are adapted to metabolize animal flesh and fat, not grains and simple sugars, including starch.*
>
> *If the natural design of dogs precludes the need for carbs, why would we feed them carbs, including grain? If their bodies aren't designed to use carbs, why would we feed them something their digestive tracts aren't equipped to process?*
>
> *I realize grain-based pet food is inexpensive and convenient. From a veterinarian's perspective, however, every day I see the consequences of feeding dogs (and cats) highly processed, biologically inappropriate food for a lifetime."*

The point:

When an animal built to eat meat consumes a grain-based diet, the result is almost always symptoms of poor health.

Looking at Legumes

Legumes are *grain free* but what many dog owners fail to realize is that legumes are still starchy-heavy. Called pulse crops, legumes are foods like beans, peas, chickpeas, peanuts, lentils, etc.

While legumes aren't toxic per se, they're known to cause digestive issues in dogs. Plus, they tend to have a high carbohydrate load and an unimpressive nutritional profile compared to fruits and vegetables.

Again, this is because they're mostly starch based.

Legumes are also *plant-based* proteins, a poor substitute for animal protein.

And as we read earlier, they're often included in pet food because legumes are cheap. This makes it easier for pet food manufacturers to game the system.

Legumes help boost the percentage of protein found in pet food formulas. But since manufacturers aren't required to share whether protein is from plant or animal sources, they're able to pull a fast one on consumers.

That's Not All: Grains and Legumes are High in Anti-Nutrients

What on earth is an anti-nutrient?

Living creatures (plants included) prefer to stay alive so they can procreate and carry on other important activities.

That's why most flora and fauna come equipped with their own personal *defense mechanisms,* called anti-nutrients.[35]

Anti-nutrients are compounds found in a variety of foods more heavily in grains and legumes. They're not all bad, but many come with unwanted health effects to discourage consumption and repel bugs and other predators.

The most predominant ailments:

1. Interference with the absorption of vitamins, minerals, digestive enzymes, and other nutrients
2. Digestive distress

There are approximately ten types of anti nutrients[36] dogs (and perhaps people) would be better off avoiding. For now, let's touch on three of the big ones in pet food:

1. Gluten
2. Phytates
3. Lectin

Gluten

Gluten is a sticky protein found in wheat, rye, bran, and barley. While it seems like a buzzword right now, the only thing you need to know is this:

Gluten is a gut *irritant*.

It's one of the most difficult-to-digest plant proteins. It's also known as an enzyme inhibitor.

Its MO: gastrointestinal distress.

Gluten can also contribute to autoimmune disease, allergic reactions or food sensitivities, leaky gut, and more. Additionally, it causes an inflammatory response, just as a cut or scrape becomes red and tender in response to an injury.

Inflammation from gluten is a problem for dogs, even if they're not gluten sensitive.

Grain-heavy diets or life-long grain consumption does one thing particularly well:

It contributes to inflammation in your dog's body, which can fuel other health issues and diseases. It can also damage their digestive tract, which is where nutrients are absorbed and the dog's resistance to disease is centered.

Phytates

Dogs lack the enzyme necessary to process phytic acid,

which is called phytase.

Phytates are infamous for binding to minerals and leeching them from your pet's body. They're known to lock up high percentages of phosphorus, calcium, copper, iron, magnesium, and zinc.

What's more, they can cause inflammation, bloating, indigestion and gas for your dog.

Phytic acid can also *inhibit* certain digestive enzymes like amylase, trypsin, and pepsin. They help your dog break down food into nutrients their bodies can absorb.

Lectins

Foods like grains and beans have especially high lectin levels.

Like most anti nutrients, lectins can reduce nutrient absorption and contribute to GI distress (namely indigestion, bloating, gas, IBS, and leaky gut).

Additionally, lectins are difficult for your dog's body to break down. They're known for their ability to survive digestion. This means they can penetrate cells lining the digestive tract, causing damage and even shift bacterial flora.

They can also trigger autoimmune reactions like joint pain, arthritis, and even rashes.

Common Allergens

Another thing to consider is that many traditional pet food ingredients are highly allergenic, especially:

• Gluten
• Soy
• Corn

The common denominator among these sticky substances is that they're all used as adhesives, either in non-food glues or as binders in the food we eat. When they're ingested, these sticky substances (some of which are waterproof) adhere to the microvilli of the intestines.

Microvilli are finger-like grabbers on the surface of the intestine. Nutrients are absorbed in the intestines, and microvilli help to amplify this process.

When the microvilli are coated with the glue proteins found in gluten, corn, and soy, many things can go awry, including:

- Reduction in the absorption of nutrients
- Microvilli damage or inflammation
- Atrophy (microvilli breaking off completely)
- Perforation of the intestinal wall

Any of the above can lead to:

- Malnourishment
- Celiac disease
- Leaky Gut
- Diabetes
- Cancer
- Arthritis
- Inflammatory Bowel Disease
- And more

Fruits and Vegetables

We're getting closer and closer to better food choices and more ancestral items. However, there are still a few things you might want to keep in mind.

Don't get me wrong:

Fruits and vegetables are vastly superior to grains and legumes, and can be *healthful* additions to a raw diet.

But plant-based foods should not make up a large part of your dog's diet, and all types of plants are not ideal for your dog.

When Too Many Fruits and Vegetables Are a Bad Thing

As we mentioned, a species-appropriate raw diet should be predominantly *meat-based*.

But as we learned, commercial dog food contains a vastly higher carbohydrate content - often around 46% to 75%. At that range, even if grains and legumes were excluded, the carbohydrate content is still too high for a meat-eating animal.

The Type of Fruits & Vegetables Included Is Just as Important

Not all plants are created equal. Plus, not all vegetables were an ancestral food item for the dog.

Wolves and other wild dogs reportedly ate grasses, sticks, bark, and mosses in the wild, along with a small percentage of seasonal fruit. Comparable vegetables and food items today might include leafy greens, herbs, and berries.

Instead, the vegetables found in pet food look like this:

- Peas
- Pumpkin
- Parsnip
- Yams
- Potatoes

The common denominator: these vegetables are *starch* heavy. And starch is a problem for your dog.

Like grains and legumes, starches can have a poor impact on your dog's gut health. They also create insulin resistance and inflammation. What's more, starches proliferate yeast throughout the body.

Yeast is a fungus that's always present on and within your dog's body.

But consider this:

A depressed immune system or a diet full of starchy foods causes this fungus to increase in the body and on hair follicles. This can lead to yeast issues and skin diseases.

Knowing that grains can contribute to this issue, pet owners rush to grab grain-free products. Pet food companies make a lot of money carrying these special diets.

Here's the problem with that solution:

What most pet owners don't know is yeast, allergies, and other skin issues aren't caused by grains alone.

Starch is a major culprit.

But here's the kicker:

Kibble cannot be made *without* starch. Starch is necessary to hold everything together; otherwise your dog's food would be a bag of dust.

So if you're feeding kibble (regardless of the kind), you're feeding starch.

And according to Dr. Karen Becker, that won't do much in the way of improving your dog's health.

> *"Replacing grains with other high-glycemic carbs won't help your dog prevent or conquer disease. It simply gives you the false sense you're feeding healthy food with a hefty price tag."*

Unfortunately, many pet parents fail to realize just how much starch (i.e. sugar) is lurking in the average bag of dog food.

What's even more troubling is pet food manufacturers don't want to show you the sugar content of their foods. If you were to ask, you're unlikely to receive a straight answer.

Why? Two reasons.

First, you need to speak in their language.

Carbohydrate is an "umbrella" term that includes all starches and sugars. These foods get converted to glucose (sugar) in the body. So don't ask about sugar because pet food manufacturers may claim there is none. Instead, ask about carbohydrates.

Second, the answer may be alarming to some pet parents.

If you want to bypass calling your pet food manufacturer, you can calculate the sugar content on your own. Filmmaker and dog food blogger, Rodney Habib coins this formula the "carb counter."[37]

Simply find the "Guaranteed Analysis" on the back of the package. Then, add protein, fat, moisture, and ash (if you can't find ash, estimate 6%). Subtract the total from 100. That will give you the percentage of carbohydrates in your dog's food.

You may be shocked to learn cheap, premium, and even grain-free dogs foods can contain up to 50% sugar.

The bottom line:

If you want to feed ancestral carbohydrates, opt for low starch, nutrient-packed vegetables and herbs instead.

What About Fruit?

Fruit can make a healthful addition to a raw diet, as long as it's fed in small quantities, as dogs don't eat too much fruit in nature.

Similar to vegetables, certain types of fruits are better suited for dogs than others; specifically, fruit with a *low sugar* content and low *glycemic* index.

Why?

Today, one in four hundred dogs have diabetes. Even more are overweight or obese, have insulin resistance, or suffer from other issues caused by an excessive carbohydrate load.

This means you should feed fewer mangos, bananas, cherries and other high-sugar fruits. Trade them in for blueberries, raspberries, blackberries, cranberries, melons, and other low-glycemic fruits instead.

Figuring Out Fats

Fat is an *essential* part of the canine diet.

Dietary fats play two key roles:

1. It provides a source of energy
2. It supplies essential fatty acids.

Fat as Fuel

Dogs (and many other carnivorous animals) use fat as a source of fuel. Unlike we're conditioned to believe, high levels of animal fats will not cause them to suffer from cholesterol problems or heart disease.

Fat is a fundamental dietary *requirement* for your dog.

Essential Fatty Acids

Dogs also depend on fat to fulfill fundamental essential fatty acid requirements. Fatty acids are a key player in a variety of important bodily functions, such as:

• Healthy skin and coat
• Reproduction
• Reducing inflammation
• Regulating an overactive immune system
• Aiding in development of the retina and visual cortex
• Prevent heart problems
• Maintaining healthy blood pressure
• Decreasing triglyceride blood cholesterol levels
• Regulating blood clotting
• Slowing development of certain types of pet cancers
• Healing
• And more

These fats are called "essential" fatty acids because dogs can't produce them on their own. They *must* come from the foods we feed.

There are two types of fatty acids we care about in dog food:

• Omega 6
• Omega 3

Dogs need both of these fats in proper balance to achieve optimal health.

The Problem with Fats in Pet Foods

Most pet foods contain more omega 6 fats than necessary while being *deficient* in omega 3s.

Traditional pet fare is made with food high in omega 6s like grains, starches, and factory-farmed meat. Animals raised on feedlots are fed cheap cereal grains full of omega 6's instead of eating grasses and other ancestral items. Because we've changed their diet, we've also changed their fatty acid composition. This means factory-farmed meat and meat byproducts are loaded with omega 6 and short in omega 3s.

Why should you care?

Too much omega 6 (and too little omega 3) throws off the precious balance of these two fats. And when your dog's consumes more omega 6's than omega 3's, it can lead to inflammation in the body.

Fatty Acid Sources Are Important Too

There are three types of omega 3 fatty acids:

1. ALA (alpha-linolenic acid)
2. DHA (docosahexaenoic acid)
3. EPA (eicosapentaenoic acid)

ALA comes from plant foods, nuts, and seeds. On the other hand, both DHA and EPA come from animal sources, mostly: fish, fish oils, eggs, and other marine sources.

Most dogs and cats get *little* DHA and EPA in their diets from traditional pet food. What's more, they're not very efficient at converting ALA into DHA or EPA.

Humans on the other hand (along with herbivores and other omnivores) can easily convert plant based ALA to EPA and DHA. Dogs can convert approximately 5-15%.

At this point, you may be noticing a theme.

Dogs do better with *animal-based* products and it's no different with fats. Fish and fish body oils are some of the best sources of omega 3s for your pet.

But they're not always available or usable in pet foods (we'll get into this more in the following chapters).

How Are Dogs Surviving Without an Ancestral Diet?

You wouldn't be the first person to ask this question.

Dogs are more resilient, enduring, and adaptable than almost any other species. Perhaps this is why it's so hard to decipher an appropriate diet. On some level, dogs were built to survive.

Dr. Karen Becker believes[38]:

> *"Dogs and cats are able to withstand significant nutritional abuse, in my opinion, without dying. Degeneration does occur as a result of an inappropriate diet but sudden death does not."*

Despite the hardiness of the dog, the facts are:

Dogs today are nutritionally weakened, suffer from degenerative diseases, chronic health issues, and have shorter lifespans.

For 99.9% of their time here on earth, dogs ate a natural diet. The other 0.1% of their time here, they've eaten a processed, non-biologically appropriate diet. It looks as if modern nutrition and westernized diets are doing a number on their health.

While the dog can certainly survive on other types of foods, the real question is:

Are they *thriving?*

Why Ancestral Foods are Important

Nature has provided a specific grouping of foods for every class of animals on the planet. Animals were built to find (hunt, graze, etc.) and consume those foods.

Each animal has a *biological predisposition* to certain foods.

Deviation from those foods is like a machine being lubricated by the wrong oil, or filled with the wrong gasoline.

Eventually, it breaks down.

This "breakdown" results in poor health and disease.

Let's move on to the next cardinal sin: dog food ingredient quality and toxicity.

Key Takeaway

Dog food ingredients have become far removed from what's species - appropriate for the dog.

10

DOG FOOD INGREDIENTS ARE OFTEN
LOW QUALITY AND POTENTIALLY TOXIC

You're a dedicated dog parent.

You listen to your veterinarian's nutritional recommendations. When shopping for pet food, you read all the labels.

Your dog eats one of the *better* brands of pet foods.

Or does he?

What most pet parents don't know is that 95% of commercially prepared dog food on the market today is made with low-quality ingredients and may contain hidden toxins.

It's about time you learned what else was lurking in your dog's food.

In this chapter, I'll outline the most important things for you to know.

Let's jump right in.

The Concept of Feed Grade

Dog owners are led to believe that pet food is made with high-quality ingredients, thanks in part to shiny advertisements and well-crafted product packaging.

In truth, most dog food on the market today contains *feed-grade* ingredients.

What's feed grade? It's a fancy way of saying junk.

It's a low quality category of food meant for animals. It's illegal to sell as "people food" because it doesn't meet human-grade quality standards.

In fact, regulatory agencies call feed-grade: "Food not fit for human consumption."

The #1 Offender: Poor Quality Protein

Let's start with animal protein.

What are some examples of feed-grade ingredients?

By-Products

This is damaged product or leftovers from human food production.

When animals are slaughtered, lean muscle is sliced off for human consumption. The waste that remains from an animal carcass is called *by-product.*

This is the protein often found in pet food.

Examples might include:

- Beaks
- Blood
- Feathers
- Wattles
- Organs like lungs, brains, or spleen
- Fatty tissue
- Frames
- Other misc. parts.

Now, *all* by-products aren't bad.

Organs are nutritious. Even bony items like chicken feet or frames can make a healthful addition to a raw diet.

But by-products omit most of the good stuff, and many have an inferior nutrient value. All in all, you're left with mostly undesirable pieces and parts.

4D Livestock

4D livestock stands for:

- Dead
- Dying
- Diseased
- Disabled

What does this mean?

"Dead" in the acronym stands for the animals that weren't *intentionally* killed in slaughter. They died beforehand, sometimes called DOA (dead on arrival). Usually due to injury, poor health, or disease.

Any animal that's dying, diseased or disabled cannot be used for human consumption. So what happens to them? They're collected to become feed-grade ingredients.

As the name 4D Livestock implies, these are usually domesticated farm animals like cows, pigs, poultry, horses, sheep, etc.

Miscellaneous Deceased or Euthanized Animals

Farm animals are not the only creatures rounded up and ground into commercial pet foods.

The mystery protein in your dog's food can also include:

- **Dogs**
- **Cats**
- Other domestic pets
- Zoo animals
- Wild animals

Yes, you read that correctly.

Dogs and cats are *not* exempt from the list of mystery meat.

How on earth is this possible?

You see, when an animal dies of natural causes or by way of euthanasia, the body has to be disposed of. Unclaimed animals are often carted away by rendering companies.

Where do they come from?

- Veterinary offices
- Animal hospitals
- Animal shelters
- Animal control
- Road kill
- Zoos

While this may sound creepy, it's a normal practice.

These types of businesses deal with a lot of animal death. Not every creature has a loving family to bury or cremate their bodies. Dead bodies have to be legally disposed of in some manner.

Grocer Waste

What do you think happens to all the unsold meat on grocery store shelves? The products that can no longer be sold to people are shipped off to rendering facilities.

This includes:

- Unsold meat
- Expired meat
- Spoiled or moldy meat
- Defective meat

While this isn't nearly as concerning as the examples above, it goes to show that pet food protein leaves much to be desired.

So How Do These Low Quality Products End up in Pet Food?

Enter *rendering*.

It's a dark and gloomy version of recycling. Quite frankly, it's the stuff nightmares are made of.

It's a process for recycling raw animal material.

Why should you care? Because rendering is the base of most pet foods and animal feeds today.

Recycled Waste Is the Base of the Pet Food Chain

I hate to say it, but the individual responsible for rendering was quite bright. He or she devised a brilliant plan to turn unsavory animal waste into profit.

Here's how it works:

Rendering plants actually provide a helpful service.

They take waste products off the hands of various businesses. By spending less time dealing with garbage, employees are able to be more productive. Some business owners even make a quick buck from the exchange.

Businesses can call rendering companies as needed, or schedule regular pick-ups. The renderer shows up and whisks away animal waste or other food production byproducts.

Sounds like a win-win for everyone, right?

Not for the dogs, cats and other animals that eat this garbage.

Food quality aside, the main reason rendered protein should be avoided is because there's a good chance it contains toxic waste.

Recycled animals waste is classified as "unfit for human consumption." It's illegal to be used for people, but can *lawfully* be used to make dog food.

You must ask yourself, "why these labels and regulations?"

Contamination is the answer.

Rendered Protein Contains More Than Animal Product

You'd think there was some kind of safety procedures at the rendering plants, right?

Wrong.

They operate haphazardly with what seems like zero concern for food safety.

Out-of-date supermarket meats, spoiled poultry, and rotten fish are trucked into rendering facilities every day.

Here's the catch:

They arrive in their original packaging. Complete with Styrofoam trays, shrink-wrap, and all. And that's exactly how they're thrown into rendering tanks.

The same goes for dead farm animals.

They go in with cattle ID tags still attached. Even deceased pets from veterinary offices and animal shelters may be tossed in vats still enclosed in waste disposal bags.

Unwrapping individual packages from the thousands of rejected grocery store products they receive each day is low priority, as is removing dead bodies from garbage bags or detaching plastic ID tags from farm animals.

Literally *anything* may be found in rendered product. Plastic, paper, Styrofoam, cardboard – it all gets hurled right into the rendering machine.

Rendered Protein Can Contain Dangerous Contaminants

Unfortunately, it gets much worse than paper, plastic, and cardboard.

Dead animals often come with a dangerous mixture of contaminants and harmful chemicals in or on their bodies. Let's look at a few common examples:

- Fish may be contaminated with *mercury* and other *heavy metals* before being thrown into vats.

- Tainted livestock can infiltrate rendered product with *pesticides.*

- *Insectide* patches, found on the skin of slaughtered

cattle and other farm animals, join the mix.

• More *insecticides* are pumped into vats as renderers throw dead pets into the grinder with flea collars still attached.

• *Metal contaminants* can infiltrate rendered product in a number of ways, most commonly through pet ID tags, pet collars, and even surgical pins and needles.

• Let's not forget potent *antibiotics* and other *pharmaceuticals* used on pets or livestock. If it's in their system, it's in the vat.

• Last but not least, the killer cocktail: Any drugs given to *euthanize* animals have regularly been found in rendered product.

I wish this was made up, but it's not.

If you're skeptical, do some research on "euthanasia drugs in pet food." You'll find no shortage of news stories and articles covering these incidents.

Sourcing the Protein Found In Pet Food

Here's another nugget to chew on:

Do you know where the meat in pet food comes from?

If you answered farms, grocery stores, the open sea, rendering facilities, or anything mentioned above - you're technically right.

But that's not the whole story.

If the information above hasn't already nauseated you, let's consider the *conditions* in which poor quality protein may be sourced.

I bet you didn't know human trafficking[39] and slave labor[40] could be part of the pet food trade. Slave labor in Thailand was responsible for the fish traced back to pet food giants Iams, Meow Mix and Fancy Feast. They were even sued[41] by consumers.

Protein Quality Deception

The courtroom is full of cases where pet food manufacturers were caught deceiving consumers about protein quality.

It's not uncommon to find "Made in the USA" claims when ingredients were sourced outside of the U.S., often in China.

Even "By-Product Free" labels were slapped on pet food packages when the opposite was proven true.

Pet food manufacturers Merrick Pet Care, Castor & Pollux, Nestle Purina, Fromm, Wyong, Alleg and even Blue Buffalo[42] have all been in the hot seat for lying to consumers.

You must understand advertising messages and even the photos on pet food packaging and are misleading. Your dog probably isn't eating chicken breast, beef chuck, or pork tenderloin.

Instead, it's more likely he's consuming recycled *waste* from human-grade food production

Don't be tricked into believing dog food is made with the same quality or cut of meat you eat at home. Or, even in the same country.

Considering protein is one of the most important nutrients for a dog, you'd think we'd want to feed quality protein.

Right?

Carbohydrate Quality Also Fails

Carbs tend to be more straightforward than animal proteins, but the issue of quality remains.

Let's start with those feed-grade ingredients again.

Plant Based By-Products

When we think of by-products, we almost always think of meat. Unsightly parts like chicken feet and beaks come to mind. But did you know there is such thing as plant-based by-products?

Here's an example:

Say you're snacking on peanuts or pistachios at home. You'd crack them open and toss the shells in the garbage.

As it turns out, those shells could be sold to pet food manufacturers and end up in your dog's kibble. Many times, the grains found in pet food are simply the product that remains *after* the grain has been processed.

They go by a variety of names:

 • **Husk or Hull** – the outer shell or coating of a seed. Commonly seen as: corn husks, oat hulls, peanut hulls, rice hulls, etc.

 • **Bran** – the hard outer layers of cereal grain. Commonly seen as: corn bran, rice bran, etc.

 • **Cellulose** – product obtained from the cell walls of a plant. It's cleaned, then mechanically processed into a fine powder. In many instances it's essentially wood pulp. Dried wood is the most common source of cellulose in food products. It's used to add bulk and consistency to pet foods. Commonly seen as: cellulose, corn cellulose, etc.

• **Mill Run** – a by-product of human food processing also referred to as "floor sweeping." This may include brans, husk, hulls, or other by production leftovers. Commonly seen as: soybean mill run, wheat mill run, etc.

It's the same with fruits and vegetables:

• **Pomace** – by-products from human food processing that don't contain all nutrients from a fresh fruit or vegetable. Commonly seen as: apple pomace, grape pomace, etc.

• **Pulp** – dried residue of a peel, pulp and seeds from citrus fruits. Commonly seen as: citrus pulp.

While these may not seem dangerous, they are insanely misleading to consumers. These ingredients are nothing more than cheap filler foods or lower quality versions of the real deal.

Pesticides Are Another Concern

This is the 21st century. I don't need to tell you pesticides are not good for your health and that you should buy *organic.*

It's the same for your dog.

Now, if you don't buy organic foods for yourself, you may not consider it a priority for your pets.

But remember, most commercial pet food is not made with organic products. It's manufactured with cheap ingredients, and these are often laced with pesticides.

Pesticides have been linked to:

• Cancer
• Obesity
• Diabetes

• Birth Defects
• And more

In fact, Roundup, the most widely used agriculture chemical in history has been a serious food contaminant for over two decades now.

According to research, the active ingredient in Roundup (glyphosate) causes leaky gut syndrome. The World Health Organization's International Agency for Research on Cancer (IARC) also announced glyphosate was a *probable* human carcinogen[43]. What's more, evidence exists that show the chemical causes cancer in lab animals and that it damages human DNA.

GMOs Are Even Worse

To understand the GMO landscape, you'd likely need to dedicate a few hours of solid research.

But here's the gist:

GMO stands for *genetically modified organism*. Like it sounds, it's an organism – in this case, plants – whose genetic makeup has been modified.

These plants were engineered to create crops resistant to pests, herbicides, or pesticides. The process has created plant genes that do not occur in nature, and (according to many) are unstable.

Studies have concluded GMOs can cause:

  • Damage to organs (liver, kidney, pancreas, reproductive organs)
  • Immune system issues
  • Changes in gut bacteria
  • Digestive disorders
  • Endocrine disruption
  • Skin and food allergies

- Cancer
- Cognitive issues
- Behavioral issues

The bottom line: GMOs have not been adequately investigated and are not proven safe.

What's worse, the US and Canada do not require labeling of genetically engineered foods, so they're tough to avoid.

That is, unless you buy *organic.*

The USDA prohibits the use of GMOs in organic foods. You can also avoid high-risk crops like corn and soy and instead focus on fruits and veggies, as most fresh produce is non-GMO.

Animal protein isn't free from GMOs either. Chances are a majority of the proteins in your pet food were fed with GMO feed.

The Mother of All Concerns: Aflatoxins

Mycotoxins are poisons produced by a fungus.

While there are many types of mycotoxins, a few are regularly found in food. One group in particular is called *aflatoxins,* and that's the one we care about.

Why?

It's considered a carcinogen.

Aflatoxins are commonly found in grains, peanut, peas, and legume products. They're especially prevalent in corn.

The molds or fungus that create aflatoxins grow in soils where conditions have to be just right.

Usually this happens through inadequate harvesting and storage. But areas with high moisture, high temperatures and piles of decomposing materials (food, plants, hay, etc.) are prime suspects.

Aflatoxins cause a number of serious health issues, including:

- Immune suppression
- Parasite infestations
- Liver enlargement
- Reduced growth rate
- Damage to offspring (aflatoxins are secreted in milk)
- Liver damage
- Liver cirrhosis
- Liver carcinoma (cancer)
- Acute necrosis (death)

Not surprisingly, liver disease is listed as the top five killers of dogs.

Kibble contains large amounts of corn, grain, pea, and legume products, most of which are poor quality and potentially contaminated. What's more, aflatoxins are *not* destroyed in the process of making pet food, and seem to survive cooking at high temperatures.

Can we possibly assume kibble is harboring aflatoxins?

That's just silly...

Or is it?

Susan Thixton, the face behind The Truth About Pet Food, initiated a consumer-funded pet food evaluation. The results[44] may shock you. The test analyzed eight pet foods for thirty-seven different mycotoxins.

Every food tested contained mycotoxins.

If that doesn't get you think differently, I don't know what will.

Let's move on to the next quality concern: fats.

Fats Can Be Recycled Too

You've probably heard enough recycling nightmares for one day. But let's learn about waste from the restaurant business.

Restaurants need to get rid of grease and frying oils from time to time. One easy solution is to have a rendering company pick up these waste products.

Where do you suppose they go? In with all the rendered protein.

This doesn't sound overly nutritious. But what's the danger in vegetable oils?

Let me explain.

Why Vegetable Oils Have No Place in a Dog's Diet

If you're not already aware, vegetable oils are not good for us. And they're not good for your *dog* either.

Here's why:

Vegetable oils are made by extracting oil from seeds. These often include soybean, rapeseed, corn, sunflower, safflower, and so on.

These oils can't be extracted through *separating* or *pressing* like butter, coconut oil or olive oil can. Instead, they must be chemically removed, deodorized, and altered.

In fact, they're some of the most chemically altered foods in the standard American diet[45]. They're often made with GMO foods doused with pesticides, and are commonly found in most processed foods on store shelves today.

What's worse, they're promoted as healthy. Yet they do

more harm than good to human and canine bodies alike.

Vegetable oil consumption can throw off the precious Omega 3:6 balance, which can cause inflammation and cell mutation. This can lead to an increased risk of cancer, autoimmune problems, intestinal damage, food allergies, and more.

The Fats in Dog Food Are Mostly Lousy

With commercial dog food, you're often getting grease, not fresh animal fat.

During the rendering process (which creates the dried protein solids used in pet food), grease or tallow rises to the top of the protein soup that's cooking.

It's skimmed off the mixture and becomes the generic "animal fat" found on the label of the average bag of dog food.

Grease is no good. It's *used* oil or fat, which tends to contain a high amount of free radicals.

In an ideal world, not only would animal fats be fresh, but also they would come from grass-fed or pastured animals with the correct balance of Omega 3:6 fats.

But as you learned, most animal protein comes from:

- By-products
- 4D livestock
- Euthanized animals
- Grocer and restaurant waste
- CAFO (concentrated animal feeding operation) livestock.

More often than not, these animals are fed cheap cereal grains and low quality animal feed. This leaves their bodies with an abundance of Omega 6 fats and a shortage of Omega 3 fats.

Disclaimer: Not All Pet Food Brands Use Low Quality Ingredients

It wouldn't be fair to say *every* pet food company uses the same low quality or toxic ingredients.

Sadly, a shocking majority does.

It seems as if the smaller or independently owned and operated companies have more freedom to source better quality ingredients. While that's not a hard and fast observation, the bigger brands have proven to be some of the worst offenders to date.

Regardless, the consumer often has no way of knowing for sure what they're getting.

As you learned, the past is riddled with instances of pet food companies that have lied, deceived, or manipulated consumers.

This doesn't mean pet food companies are *evil*.

It means there's something wrong with the status quo. In our society, pet food is viewed differently than people food. It sits far below human fare on the totem pole of quality.

All living creatures need real, fresh, quality foods to thrive.

Kibble With Human Grade Ingredients

There are well-intentioned pet food companies that source higher quality ingredients, or even *human-grade* ingredients on the market today.

But this leads to the next issue: processing.

Pet food is so heavily processed that even responsible brands making use of high-quality ingredients can fall way short.

Let's learn more about this mysterious process called rendering and glimpse into the world of pet food production. Ready?

Key Takeaway:

A majority of commercial wet and dry dog foods contain hidden toxins and chemicals.

11 DOG FOOD IS HEAVILY PROCESSED

Here's the brutal truth about dog food manufacturing:

The ingredients alone can be frightening, but at the end of the process, there's little left that resembles *real* food.

While some dog owners have no clue how pet food is made, others would rather remain in the dark. Chances are, they've heard some unsettling rumors.

I get that. We all want to sleep better at night.

But if you're serious about providing better quality nutrition for your dog, you need to know exactly what they're eating *and* how it's made.

Only then can make better decisions about what to feed.

Rendering and Extrusion

There are two processes involved in about 95% of kibble production. They're usually carried out by two separate, independent businesses.

One is in the business of recycling to create raw materials. The other uses these raw materials in their products.

These processes are called:

1. Rendering
2. Extrusion

Let's dive right in.

Rendering Defined

You've learned a lot about the ingredients used in the rendering process, but not much about what actually happens at a rendering plant.

Rendering is an industrial process "that converts waste animal tissue into stable, value-added materials."[46]

In plain English, here's what happens:

Animal product is dumped into large vats, ground into smaller pieces, cooked for hours at extreme temperatures, then screened or sifted to separate substances into end products.

The rendering process eliminates moisture from raw product and separates fat from both bone and protein.

This creates two products:

1. Fat product (typically yellow grease)
2. Protein meal (meat and bone meal).[47]

The final products are routinely sold as a source of protein meal and fat for making pet foods and animal feeds.

There are many rendering plants scattered throughout the world. They operate like giant commercial kitchens, except without health inspections or reasonable food safety protocols.

An Average Day at a Rendering Facility

To start, raw animal product is trucked in[48] and unloaded onto concrete dump areas.

At many rendering facilities, these concrete slabs are sloped away from main buildings. This allows workers to wash down surfaces (because as you might imagine, these areas become covered in filth).

Dead animals begin to pile up in the thousands: dogs and cats; heads, hooves, and other pieces from cattle, sheep, goats, and horses; even road kill like skunks, rats, and raccoons.

Carcasses and various body parts sit in piles waiting to be rendered, often baking in the sun for hours.

Accounts from workers, plant inspectors and even neighboring families describe the smell as foul, horrendous, and nauseating.[49] [50] [51]

If that hasn't trigger your gag reflex yet, this might help:

The rotting carcasses are often overwhelmed with pests: rats, flies, and maggots.

Visitors have claimed piles of animal product in concrete dumping areas tend to take on a life of their own. Infested and swarming with maggots, it almost looks as if the carcasses are moving.

In the Vat They Go

Next, Bobcats haul loads of animal carcasses inside the plant and drop them into a rendering pit. This vat is essentially a deep, dark concrete hole with slanted sides.

Because most rendering facilities have pest problems, seams in the concrete pits may contain rat holes. In many facilities, you can see rats living in the rendering pit.

While I'd love to tell you that everything chucked into that lifeless pit was indeed lifeless, that's not always the case.

Witnesses have attested to some inhumane practices.

One account in particular told of chickens being delivered in the dumping area – some still alive, staggering around, sick and dying. These chickens were picked up and thrown in the vat to be ground alive.

What Happens Inside the Pit

A giant auger at the bottom grinds carcasses into smaller pieces. Let's just say the sounds of popping bones and squeezing flesh are not something any first-hand witness had fun recounting.

Once the carcasses are ground into smaller pieces, another auger may be used for finer shredding. After this step is complete, off the remains go to be cooked at high temperatures for an hour or more.

This batch cooking process operates around the clock, melting meat away from bones. Throughout the process, the fat is skimmed off the top of this hot soup.

It's Hammer Time

Afterwards, cooked meat and bone are sent to a hammer-mill press. Its job: squeezing out moisture and pulverizing product into a gritty powder.

Next, shaker screens sift excess hair, large bone chips and other inedible items: concrete fragments, metals, or anything else that survived the cooked process.

All that's left is yellow grease and a meat and bone meal product. It's packaged, then shipped to pet food and animal feed manufacturers.

The Difference Between Rendering and Pet Food Production

Rendering is what comes *before* pet food.

The rendering process creates the raw materials used by pet food companies in their own pet food formulas.

Here's a real life example:

A bakery doesn't make flour or sugar. They buy those ingredients, which go into the baked goods they create. It's the same with pet food. Pet food manufacturers buy protein and bone meal to use as the protein base or fat additive in their own recipes.

Pet Food Production

It all starts with a recipe formulated by the pet food company. This recipe is handed off to an animal food manufacturer, where they carry out the cooking, mixing, and bagging of pet food product.

Pet food is generally made through a process known as *extrusion*. It's a fancy name for a complicated process.

Make no mistake; kibble production is not like baking dog biscuits at home. The end result is quite different than the original ingredients used in the recipe.

So what exactly happens at the kibble factory?

Dry Ingredients

First, a massive quantity of dry ingredients are purchased by the truckload and usually stored in silos.

These dry ingredients are run through a machine called a hammer mill.

This machine grinds product to a precise size, often comparable to coarse flour. Much like sifting dry ingredients when baking, this creates a uniform consistency to ensure the proper absorption of water and correct cooking times.

Mixing Wet and Dry Ingredients

Next, the various ingredients are blended together.

This is typically achieved with a machine called a ribbon mixer. It uses computers to generate exact proportions of each ingredient.

The mixture must be "pre-conditioned" before moving onto the next step. Pre-conditioning mixes wet and dry ingredients together, creating a dough-like consistency. Wet ingredients vary, but can include fats, oils, water and steam.

The scorching hot water and pressurized steam begin the cooking process. This is when starches start to gelatinize (in other words, melt). This serves to bind the kibble together and help with expansion in the next step of the production process.

The Dough Takes Shape

In the fourth step, the dough is fed into a machine called an expander, more commonly known as an *extruder.*

An extruder machine is big, bulky, and looks like something that belongs in a science lab and not a commercial kitchen. These machines were originally designed for the plastics[52] industry.

The extruder features a long metal tube with a giant screw inside. Dough is fed in one end and propelled forward with the internal screw.

Once it reaches the other side, it's pushed through something called a *die.* Think of a die like a cookie cutter, it determines the shape of the kibble.

The tube walls are heated to extreme temperatures so that the dough cooks as it touches the internal walls and is driven forward. There's also an insane amount of pressure inside this metal tube, which contributes to the high temperature of the dough.

Once the dough makes its way to the end of the extruder tube, it's forced through the die and sliced free.

As soon as it hits open air, the pressure releases. This causes the precooked dough to expand by about 50%. These hot, soft, and puffed-up kibble pieces are now ready for the final step.

Time for Drying and Additives

The fifth step of this painstaking process is called *enrobing.*

Here, the food goes into dryers to harden. Next, it's sprayed with synthetic nutrients and doused in flavor enhancing liquids or powders, along with other additives.

After the spraying, there's another round of drying. Then

the newly created kibble nuggets are rushed to bagging before the fats, oils and other ingredients can spoil.

Finally, it's weighed and shipped out to your nearest pet store.

So What's Wrong with Processed Dog Food?

Here are the three biggest issues with heavily processed pet foods:

1. Moisture Loss
2. Nutrient Destruction
3. Chemical Additives

Let's address all three.

Processed Food Lacks Moisture

Animals don't strut around with high-tech or trendy water bottles. They don't strive to drink eight glasses of water per day, either.

Why do they seem to drink less than us?

Because most animals get water from the foods they eat, rather than drinking water by itself.

Food in the wild – natural, raw foods – are *moisture* dense. Take the human body, for instance. It's 60% water. Muscles and kidneys are 79% water, and even our bones are 31% water.

For carnivores, their prey is mostly water. In fact, an ancestral diet for dogs can contain up to 70% water.

Let's compare that to kibble.

Dry, processed dog foods contain approximately **12% moisture.**

This gives a new meaning to the term bone dry. Kibble has less than half of the moisture content than human bones.

Why is water so important?

- It aids in the digestion of food and helps move food through the digestive tract.
- Water carries and moves important nutrients into and out of the cells in the body.
- It helps the body absorb nutrients.
- Water cools the body and assists in maintaining a normal body temperature.
- It lubricates and cushions joints, making movement easier.
- Other tissues, including the spinal cord, are cushioned by water.
- Waste is removed from the body with the help of water through urination and bowel movements.

Just about every important bodily function requires water.

Without proper water intake, your dog can become dehydrated. This can lead to organ damage. If chronic dehydration lasts long enough, your dog's organs will begin to shut down.

Needless to say, water is vital in the foods your dog eats.

When your dog eats kibble, he's running on a water *shortage* – and unfortunately, not all dogs drink enough to make up for this what's missing in their food.

This leads me to the next processing peril:

Nutrient Destruction

Raw foods are *nutrient dense*.

They contain the largest concentration of vitamins, minerals and enzymes. This is because raw food is essentially alive.

When food is cooked, there's usually some degree of nutrient loss that occurs in the process. Some cooking methods are better than others at preserving vital nutrients, but the more we process a food, the more we lose.

With processed pet food, nutrients can be almost destroyed.

All forms of kibble share one thing in common, regardless of the quality of ingredients used. After all the heating, cooking, and processing – there's little left for your dog to *live* on.

Most of the ingredients in the average bag of kibble are processed six or seven times before bags hit store shelves.

Don't believe me? Let's count together:

1. Rendering – raw animal material or "protein" is processed at least once, possibly twice. It's cooked at temperatures hovering around 280 degrees, often for hours at a time.

2. Hammer Mill – Dry ingredients including meat and bone meal are grinded into a flour-like powder. Animals, meat and bone have been heated, melted, and processed so intensely that they are now in the form of flour.

3. Preconditioning – Hot water and pressurized steam cook the ingredients.

4. Extruder – Tube walls reaching extremely high temperatures cook ingredients as they're pushed through the steel cylinder.

5. Enrobing Round One– After kibble is sliced from the die, it goes into a heated oven to dry and harden.

6. Enrobing Round Two – After being sprayed with other liquids and powers, the kibble goes back into the heated oven for the final phase of drying and hardening.

Kibble opponents argue that roughly *half* the nutrition is baked out of your dog's food every time it's heated.

When ingredients are heated five or six times throughout the entire process, it's safe to assume what nutrients may have been present in the food are now lost.

Here Comes Fake Nutrition

After all the pulverizing, processing, cooking, and preserving in kibble production, there's *little* nutrition left in pet food. The pet food company knows this.

Understanding their foods are highly deficient, they have to do something to compensate for this.

Here's what's sly:

They add vitamins and minerals back to their food.

But it's *fake*, synthetic nutrition.

Not only are fake vitamins and minerals not good enough for your dog, but synthetic vitamins and minerals:

• Aren't easily absorbed by the body
• Are less shelf-stable and can be destroyed during storage or shipping
• Are less effective
• Are unpredictable and can cause an increased risk of cancer and other health issues

Vitamins are defined as "a group of complex organic compounds." This means that they work in synergy together.

Synthetic vitamins are different.

Here's why:

First, they're not natural.

They're made in labs owned by pharmaceutical companies, many of which are located in China. This alone is frightening, because China has a poor track record with food safety.

Second, a synthetic vitamin contains a *fraction* of what's found in naturally occurring vitamins.

According to the experts, synthetic vitamins are "missing important cofactors that make them work." Time and time again, studies have shown natural vitamins have a larger impact on health compared to synthetic vitamins.

Clearly, synthetic vitamins can't hold a candle to the real thing. But what happens to dogs that consume a lifetime of fake nutrients?

Why Synthetic is a Problem For Your Dog

If your dog eats processed pet food, he's relying on synthetic nutrients for a majority of his nutrition.

But your dog can't live on nutrient-depleted foods for very long *without* developing chronic disease.

Your dog needs nutrients to fuel the cells in his body. Over time, nutritional deficiencies can break down your dog's cells and eventually his body. It starts with immune system suppression and can grow to chronic inflammation, organ failures, and eventually disease.

Proper nutrition is key to health and longevity.

So when it comes to nutrients like vitamins, minerals, and enzymes for your dog, it's better to rely on the ones nature created.

Chemical Additives

Aside from synthetic nutrition, there's an abundance of other chemicals sprayed on at the end of the kibble production process.

Let's recap a few of these:

1. **Palatability enhancers**, a coating of fats, oils and other chemicals to coax your dog into eating food he would otherwise turn his nose up at.

2. **Coloring agents,** to create an artificial "rich and meaty" look to appeal to dog owners. These food dyes have been linked[53] to carcinogens and a range of other health issues (allergic reactions, behavioral issues, and tumors).

3. **Sweeteners and flavoring agents** to make the pet food taste better. Not only are these sugary agents *not* ancestral or necessary, they can also be addictive and cause health issues like allergies, yeast, skin issues, obesity, diabetes, cataracts, tooth decay, arthritis, and can feed cancers.

Fat Safety Concerns

Fats are *delicate.*

When fat is exposed to the air or high temperatures, it spoils rapidly. Long-term consumption of rancid fats is not healthy for people or dogs.

One of two things can happen:

1. Fat can spoil with the high temperatures used in the cooking process.

2. If they haven't, the fats in dog food will likely spoil as soon as a bag of dog food is opened and exposed to the air.

Because the high temperatures at which kibble is cooked destroys nutrients, synthetic vitamins and minerals are added afterwards to beef up the nutrient content of the food.

Many times, this nutrient mix consists of a lot of metal oxides and sulfates that promote the *oxidation* of fat. This can cause the pet food to become unbalanced.

What you may not know is that *chemical reactions* are taking place inside your bag of dog food. That reaction can become amplified the longer it sits, or if it's in a hot environment. Once the bag is opened, the fats may go rancid.[54]

Rancid fats can react with synthetic metals, causing oxidation. This may lead to opportunistic bacteria and mycotoxins.

As you learned in the last chapter, mycotoxins are a toxic substance caused by fungus. And we already saw that they were present in a number of commercial pet foods.

Pet food companies claim kibble is complete, balanced, and shelf stable.

As you can see, that's just not true...

A healthier choice for your dog: fresh fats in their natural state, or added as an addition to food at mealtime – fish oils, for example.

Preservatives

By definition, a preservative is "a substance or chemical that is added to products such as food... to prevent decomposition by microbial growth or by undesirable chemical changes."

Preservatives are found in all dry and wet pet foods. It's what stops them from *spoiling* and makes them shelf stable.

As we learned above, fats are delicate and prone to spoilage. Knowing this, pet food manufacturers must add preservatives to many fat and oil products.

While there are a wide range of preservatives used in pet food today, let's talk about the foul four that should *never* be fed to any pet.

1. BHA (Butylated Hydroxyanisole)

2. BHT (Butylated Hydroxytoluene)

Both BHA and BHT are common chemicals added to preserve oils and fats.

The World Health Organization named these chemicals as suspicious cancer-causing compounds. California's Office of Environmental Health Hazard Assessment added this to the list of *known* carcinogens and reproductive toxins.

BHT is also linked to kidney and liver damage in rats. Despite this, these two nasty chemical preservatives are allowed in pet food.

3. Ethoxyquin

Ethoxyquin is used as a preservative, as a pesticide, and as a hardening agent for synthetic rubber.

Human safety data reports claim Ethoxyquin is harmful if swallowed or if in direct contact with the skin. It's also been under investigation by the FDA as a possible cause for liver and blood problems.

It's illegal to use in human foods in the US, but legal for pet foods.

Other countries have more sense. Ethoxyquin is not permitted for use in Australian dog foods or in the

European Union.

4. PG (Propylene Glycol)

This is a moistening agent and is chemically derived from glycol (EG), also known as *antifreeze*. If you don't know already, antifreeze is extremely toxic to animals

I shouldn't have to say this, but I don't recommend you feed antifreeze derivatives to your pets.

Wrapping It All Up

There you have it – an overview of the horrors found in the production of pet food.

The rendering process is grotesque and unsanitary at best. Extrusion involves so much heavy processing that food is left devoid of water and nutrients. To top it off, pet food is chock full of dangerous chemicals.

It's safe to say processed pet food is not all it's cracked up to be.

For those of you still uncertain if it's really *that* bad, let me leave you with one last piece of evidence.

At study by Dr. Kollath in Stockholm, Sweden followed dogs on a processed diet and dogs on a raw diet.

The conclusion:

The dogs on a processed diet appeared healthy, then rapidly aged and developed degenerative disease symptoms. The raw fed group aged slower, were healthier, and showed no degenerative disease symptoms.[55]

Another study conducted in Belgium[56] followed dogs on a homemade diet consisting of high-quality foods versus dogs fed commercially prepared pet food.

The conclusion:

Dogs on the high-quality homemade diet had a life expectancy of approximately three years longer

The bottom line:

Commercial wet and dry pet foods are a toxic food product. Choose fresh, raw, wholesome foods instead, and give your dog *life.*

Key Takeaway:

Traditional dog food is so heavily processed that the end product offers little value.

"The food you eat either makes you more healthy or less healthy. Those are your options"

-Dallas & Melissa Hartwig

THERE'S A BETTER WAY

If you want your dog to live a long and healthy life, then you have to make a change.

Let nature be your guide.

Feed the foods your dog was designed to eat. Ditch processed, fake, toxic and chemical-infused junk.

Favor fresh, raw foods instead.

Imagine a life where your dog is full of energy, vitality, and vigor. Picture shiny coats, a health body condition, and an overall happier animal. Look into the future and see your dog aging gracefully.

Believe it or not, more time with your dog is in the realm of possibility.

That is, if you put health first.

Sure, it sounds scary...

But you're capable of this. You care for yourself and your family and you too can better care for your dog.

And I'll be with you every step of the way.

Stop overthinking it and try a raw diet today. You and your dog have nothing to lose and everything to gain.

Footnotes

1. Wolf Food

[1] Wikipedia, *Carinvore*, 2004
<https://en.wikipedia.org/wiki/Carnivore>

[2] Living With Wolves, *How Wolves Hunt*, 2014, LivingWithWolves. org <https://www.livingwithwolves.org/how-wolves-hunt/>

[3] Defenders of Wildlife, *Basic Facts About Gray Wolves*, 2015, Defenders.org <https://defenders.org/gray-wolf/basic-facts>

[4] Mary Montgomery, *Gray Wolf*, 2009 https://www.macalester.edu/~montgomery/graywolf.html>

[5] The National Wildlife Federation, *Gray Wolf*, NWF.org <https://www.nwf.org/Educational-Resources/Wildlife-Guide/ Mammals/Gray-Wolf>

[6] International Wolf Center, Wolf FAQ's, 2015, Wolf.org <http://www.wolf.org/wolf-info/basic-wolf-info/wolf-faqs/#r>

[7] Raincoast Conservation Foundation, *Spawning salmon disrupt tight trophic coupling between wolves and ungulate prey in coastal British Columbia*, 2008, Raincoast.org <https://www.raincoast. org/2008/11/spawning-salmon-disrupt-tight-trophic-coupling-between-wolves-and-ungulate-prey-in-coastal-british-columbia/>

2. Evolution of the Wolf

[8] Nikolai D. Ovodov, Susan J. Crockford, Yaroslav V. Kuzmin , Thomas F. G. Higham, Gregory W. L. Hodgins, Johannes van der Plicht, *'A 33,000-Year-Old Incipient Dog from the Altai Mountains of Siberia: Evidence of the Earliest Domestication Disrupted by the Last Glacial Maximum'*, PLOS One (2011)

[9] Elizabeth Landau, *Dogs first domesticated in Europe Study Says*, 2013, CNN.com <https://www.cnn.com/2013/11/14/health/dogs-domesticated-europe/>

[10] PBS, *Dogs That Changed the World: What caused the domestication of wolves?*, 2011, PBS.org <http://www.pbs.org/ wnet/nature/dogs-that-changed-the-world-what-caused-the-domestication-of-wolves/1276/>

[11] Brian Hare,Vanessa Woods, Opinion: *We Didn't Domesticate Dogs. They Domesticated Us*, 2013, NationalGeographic.com <https://news.nationalgeographic.com/news/2013/03/130302-dog-domestic-evolution-science-wolf-wolves-human/>

[12] Hannah Harris, *How Dogs Work*, 2006, HowStuffWorks.com <https://animals.howstuffworks.com/pets/dog.htm>

3. Domestication of the Dog

[13] Marshall Brain, *How Evolution Works*, 2001, HowStuffWorks. com <https://science.howstuffworks.com/life/evolution/evolution. htm>

[14] Annenberg Learner, *Life Science: Session 5 - Artificial Selection at Work*, 2009, Learner.org <https://www.learner.org/courses/essential/life/session5/closer1.html>

[15] American Museum of Natural History, *What is Domestication?*, 2015, AMNH.org <https://www.amnh.org/exhibitions/horse/domesticating-horses/what-is-domestication>

4. Animal Classification, Simplified

[16] Wikipedia, *Taxonomy (biology)*, 2013, Wikipedia.org <https://en.wikipedia.org/wiki/Taxonomy_(biology)>

6. Are Dogs Carnivores or Omnivores?

[17] Erik Axelsson, Abhirami Ratnakumar, Maja-Louise Arendt, Khurram Maqbool, Matthew T. Webster, Michele Perloski, Olof Liberg, Jon M. Arnemo, Åke Hedhammar & Kerstin Lindblad-Toh, *'The genomic signature of dog domestication reveals adaptation to a starch-rich diet'*, Nature, 495, 360 (2013)

[18] Prescott Deininger, *What does the fact that we share 95 percent of our genes with the chimpanzee mean? And how was this number derived?*, Scientific American, 2004 <https://www.scientificamerican.com/article/what-does-the-fact-that-w/>

[19] Dr Doug Knueven, DVM, *Research Proves It: Dogs Thrive on a Starch-Rich Diet*, 2013, DogsNaturallyMagazine.com <http://www.dogsnaturallymagazine.com/research-proves-it-dogs-thrive-on-a-starch-rich-diet/>

[20] Landry SM, Van Ruining HJ, *The diet of feral carnivores: a review of stomach content analysis* (J Am Animal Hosp Assoc. 1979).

[21] Coppinger R, Coppinger L. *Dogs: A Startling New Understanding of Canine Origin, Behavior & Evolution* (New York, Simon & Schuster, 2001).

[22] Puotinen CJ, *What a wolf eats: research on wild canids can help inform dietary planning for dogs* (Whole Dog Journal, 2005)

[23] David L Mech and Luigi Boitani, *Wolves: Behavior, Ecology, and Conservation* (Chicago: The University of Chicago Press, 2003).

[24] David L Mech and Luigi Boitani, *Wolves: Behavior, Ecology, and Conservation* (Chicago: The University of Chicago Press, 2003).

[25] Wikipedia, *Carinvore*, 2004, Wikipedia.org <https://en.wikipedia.org/wiki/Carnivore>

8. Welcome to the Age of Pet Food Advertising

[26] Donald G. McNeil JR., INTERNATIONAL BUSINESS: *A Diamond Cartel May Be Forever; The Hereditary Leader of De Beers Pursues Post-Apartheid Growth*, Jan. 12, 1999, NYTimes.com <https://www.nytimes.com/1999/01/12/business/international-business-diamond-cartel-may-be-forever-hereditary-leader-de-beers.html>

[27] Wikipedia, Spratt's, 2011, Wikipedia.org <https://en.wikipedia.org/wiki/Spratt's>

9. Dog Food Ingredients Are Not Always Biologically Appropriate

[28] National Research Council, *Nutrient Requirements of Dogs and Cats* (Washington, DC., The National Academies Press, 2006).

[29] The Association of American Feed Control Officials, *AAFCO Dog and Cat Food Nutrient Profiles*, 2014 , Petfood.aafco.org <https://www.aafco.org/Portals/0/SiteContent/Regulatory/Committees/Pet-Food/Reports/Pet_Food_Report_2013_Midyear-Proposed_Revisions_to_AAFCO_Nutrient_Profiles.pdf>

[30] Linda P. Case, Leighann Daristotle, Michael G. Hayek, Melody Foess Raasch, *Canine and Feline Nutrition: A Resource for Companion Animal Professionals* (Maryland Heights, Missouri: Mosby Elsevier, 2011).

[31] Michael S. Hand, Craig D. Thatcher, Rebecca L. Remillard, Philip Roudebush, Lon D. Lewis, *Small Animal Clinical Nutrition*, 4th Edition (Mark Morris Institute; 2000)

[32] I.H. Burger, *The Waltham Book of Companion Animal Nutrition*, 2nd Edition (Butterworth-Heinemann; 1993)

[33] John Robbins, *The Truth About Grassfed Beef*, FoodRevolution. org <https://foodrevolution.org/blog/the-truth-about-grassfed-beef/>

[34] Dr. Karen Becker, *Don't Fall for the 'Grain-Free' Trick Pulled by Some Pet Food Makers*, 2016, HealthyPets.Mercola.com <https://healthypets.mercola.com/sites/healthypets/ archive/2016/12/12/dogs-grain-free-diet.aspx>

[35] Mark Sisson, *Why Grains are Unhealthy*, 2009, MarksDailyApple. com <https://www.marksdailyapple.com/why-grains-are-unhealthy/>

[36] Dr. Josh Axe, 10 *Antinutrients to Get Out of Your Diet...and Life*, 2015, DrAxe.com <https://draxe.com/antinutrients/>

[37] Rodney Habib, *Grain-Free & Prescription Dog Food vs "The Cheapest Dog Food"*, 2017 <https://www.facebook.com/ PlanetPaws.ca/videos/1289806047760941/>

[38] Dr. Karen Becker, *The Feeding Mistake Linked to the Cause of Most Disease - Are You Making It?*, 2013, HealthyPets.Mercola. com <https://healthypets.mercola.com/sites/healthypets/ archive/2013/04/01/raw-food-diet-part-1.aspx>

10. Dog Food Ingredients Are Often Low Quality and Potentially Toxic

[39] John Haltiwanger, *The Ugly Truth Behind Your Pet's Food And Its Connection To Slave Labor*, 2015, EliteDaily.com <https://www. elitedaily.com/news/politics/pets-food-slave-labor-connection-thai-fishing-boats/1147060>

[40] Ian Urbina, *'Sea Slaves': The Human Misery That Feeds Pets and Livestock*, 2015, NYTimes.com <https://www.nytimes. com/2015/07/27/world/outlaw-ocean-thailand-fishing-sea-slaves-pets.html?_r=0>

[41] Susan Thixton, *Pet Food Consumers Sue Fancy Feast for alleged use of Slave Labor Ingredients*, 2015, TheTruthAboutPetFood.com <http://truthaboutpetfood.com/pet-food-consumers-sue-fancy-feast-for-using-slave-labor-ingredients/>

[42] JC Torpey, *Purina Vs. Blue Buffalo Lawsuit: Blue Admits Pet Food Contains Chicken, Poultry Byproduct*, 2015, Inquisitr.com <http://www.inquisitr.com/2093177/purina-vs-blue-buffalo-lawsuit-blue-admits-pet-food-contains-chicken-poultry-byproduct/>

[43] World Health Organization International Agency for Research on Cancer, *IARC Monographs Volume 112: evaluation of five organophosphate insecticides and herbicides*, 2015, IARC.fr <https://www.iarc.fr/en/media-centre/iarcnews/pdf/MonographVolume112.pdf>

[44] Susan Thixton, *The Pet Food Test Results*, 2015, TheTruthAboutPetFood.com <http://truthaboutpetfood.com/the-pet-food-test-results/>

[45] Katie Wells, *Why You Should Never Eat Vegetable Oil or Margarine*, 2014, WellnessMama.com <https://wellnessmama.com/2193/never-eat-vegetable-oil/>

11. Dog Food Is Heavily Processed

[46] Wikipedia, *Rendering (animal products)*, 2014, Wikipedia.org <https://en.wikipedia.org/wiki/Rendering_(animal_products)>

[47] Wikipedia, *Meat and bone meal*, 2004, Wikipedia.org <https://en.wikipedia.org/wiki/Meat_and_bone_meal>

[48] Dr. Judy Morgan, *Spoiled, Unrefrigerated Meats Used for Pet Food*, 2016, DrJudyMorgan.com <http://www.drjudymorgan.com/spoiled-meats-pet-food/>

[49] Steve Orr, Meaghan McDermott, *What's that Smell? Homeowners say odor affecting quality of life*, 2014, DemocratAndChronicle.com <https://www.democratandchronicle.com/story/news/2014/08/30/penfiled-baker-commodities-rendering-smell/14830513/>

[50] CTV Montreal, *RDP Residents Struggle to Cope with Rendering Plant's Strong Odour*, 2016, Montreal.CTVNews.ca <https://montreal.ctvnews.ca/rdp-residents-struggle-to-cope-with-rendering-plant-s-strong-odour-1.2979662>

[51] Kate McGillivray, *Animal Rendering Plant Causing Horrible Smell RDP Resident says*, 2016, CBC.ca<http://www.cbc.ca/news/canada/montreal/sanimax-smell-rdp-1.3668726>

[52] Wikipedia, *Plastics extrusion*, 2006, Wikipedia.org <https://en.wikipedia.org/wiki/Plastics_extrusion>

[53] Center For Science in the Public Interest, *Food Dyes: A Rainbow of Risks*, 2010, Cspinet.org <https://cspinet.org/new/pdf/food-dyes-rainbow-of-risks.pdf>

[54] Steve Brown, *Unlocking the Canine Ancestral Diet* (Wenatchee, Washington: Dogwise Publishing, 2010)

[55] Roxanne Stone MSc, *'Kibble: Why It's Not A Good Option For Your Dog'*, DogsNaturallyMagazine.com, 2012 <http://www.dogsnaturallymagazine.com/kibble-never-a-good-option/>

[56] Dr. Gerard Lippert, *Relation between the domestic dogs' well-being and life expectancy statistical essay*, 2003 <http://www.ukrmb.co.uk/images/LippertSapySummary.pdf

Your Eyes are Open. Now What?

For pet parents wondering where to go from here, the answer is simple. Forward! Amy's website, PrimalPooch. com, offers guidance for pet parents interested in continuing to learn about raw feeding.

Free Raw Feeding Education

PrimalPooch.com offers a comprehensive framework for feeding your dog a raw diet. You'll find in-depth, educational articles and definitive guides on a variety of raw feeding topics. Within her content, Amy leaves no stone unturned, answering all of your questions, offering step-by- step directions, and encouraging her blog readers to action.

Raw Dog Food Recommendations

Sourcing items for a canine raw diet can be a challenge when first starting out. PrimalPooch.com also features advice on raw diet products and supplies, and where to buy them. Amy makes it easy for her readers by offering everything you need in one place, including brand recommendations and advice.

Your journey into the world of raw feeding doesn't have to stop here. Visit Amy's website for a wealth of information on raw feeding, or get in touch with her at amy@primalpooch.com.

Made in the USA
Middletown, DE
26 January 2022

58604130R00086